M000240305

PEMBROKE WELSH CORGI AND CORGIS

Pembroke Welsh Corgi Total Guide

PEMBROKE WELSH CORGI, CORGI PUPPIES, CORGI PUPPIES FOR SALE, PEMBROKE WELSH CORGI BREEDERS, PEMBROKE WELSH CORGI TRAINING, HEALTH, HISTORY & MORE!

Susanne Saben

© DYM Worldwide Publishers

DYM Worldwide Publishers

ISBN: 978-1-911355-85-4

Copyright ©2018 DYM Worldwide Publishers, 2018
2 Lansdowne Row, Number 240 London W1J 6HL

ALL RIGHTS RESERVED. This book contains material protected under International & Federal Copyright Laws & Treaties. Any unauthorized reprint or use of this material is strictly prohibited. No part of this book may be reproduced or transmitted in any form or by any means, electronic, mechanical, or otherwise, including photocopying or recording, or by any information storage or retrieval system without express written permission from the author.

Published by DYM Worldwide Publishers 2018.

Copyright and Trademarks. This publication is Copyright 2018 by DYM Worldwide Publishers. All products, publications, software, and services mentioned and recommended in this publication are protected by trademarks. In such instance, all trademarks & copyright belonging to the respective owners. All rights reserved. No part of this book may be reproduced or transferred in any form or by any means, graphic, electronic, or mechanical, including but not limited to photocopying, recording, taping, scanning, or by any information storage retrieval system, without the written permission of the author. Pictures used in this book are royalty free pictures purchased from stock photo websites with full rights for use within this work.

Disclaimer and Legal Notice. This product is not legal or medical advice and should not be interpreted in that manner. You need to do your own due diligence to determine if the content of this product is right for you. The author, publisher, distributors, and or/affiliates of this product are not liable for any damages or losses associated with the content of this product. While every attempt has been made to verify the information shared in this publication, neither the author, publisher, distributors, and/or affiliates assume any responsibility for errors, omissions, or contrary interpretation of the subject matter herein. Any perceived slights to any specific person(s) or organization(s) are purely unintentional. We have no control over the nature, content, and availability of the websites listed in this book.

The inclusion of any website links does not necessarily imply a recommendation or endorse the views expressed within them.

DYM Worldwide Publishers takes no responsibility for, and will not be liable for, the websites being temporarily or being removed from the Internet. The accuracy and completeness of the information provided herein, and opinions stated herein are not guaranteed or warranted to produce any particular results, and the advice or strategies, contained herein may not be suitable for every individual. The author, publisher, distributors, and/or affiliates shall not be liable for any loss incurred as a consequence of the use and application, directly or indirectly of any information presented in this work. This publication is designed to provide information regarding the subject matter covered. The information included in this book has been compiled to give an overview of the topics covered. The information contained in this book has been compiled to provide an overview of the subject. It is not intended as medical advice and should not be construed as such. For a firm diagnosis of any medical conditions, you should consult a doctor or veterinarian (as related to animal health). The writer, publisher, distributors, and/or affiliates of this work are not responsible for any damages or negative consequences following any of the treatments or methods highlighted in this book.

Website links are for informational purposes only and should not be seen as a personal endorsement; the same applies to any products or services mentioned in this work. The reader should also be aware that although the web links included were correct at the time of writing they may become out of date in the future. Any pricing or currency exchange rate information was accurate at the time of writing but may become out of date in the future. The Author, Publisher, distributors, and/or affiliates assume no responsibility for pricing and currency exchange rates mentioned within this work.

Foreword

What has four short stubby legs, big pointy ears, and endless energy and love to give? The Pembroke Welsh Corgi! These little dogs are an absolute joy to be around and, if you're lucky enough to own one, you'll find that they make the very best of companions. I am the fortunate owner of a 4-year-old Corgi myself, and she is the light of my life and has been since I got her.

While the Pembroke Welsh Corgi may look a little odd compared to other dogs, I prefer to think of them as unique. They are smart and goofy, outgoing and friendly, plus they are extremely affectionate. My kids love our Lucy, and she is an important part of our family. I can't imagine living my life without her!

Before I got Lucy, I was slightly familiar with the Corgi breed – I knew they had short legs but could run remarkably fast. What I didn't know is that they are also some of the sweetest and most playful dogs out there.

Once Lucy came into my life, I knew I had to share my joy with others, so I set out to write this book. In these pages, you'll find a wealth of knowledge about the Pembroke Welsh Corgi breed and its care to help you determine whether this is the right breed for you. If you decide that it is, you'll also find all the practical information you need to get started as a Corgi owner.

So, if you're ready to keep learning about what makes the Pembroke Welsh Corgi so wonderful, just turn the page and keep reading!

Table of Contents

Chapter 1 – Introduction..10
Useful Terms to Know...13
Chapter 2 – Introduction to the Pembroke Welsh Corgi 17
1.) Pembroke Welsh Corgi History.......................19
2.) Interesting Facts about the Corgi Dog Breed 21
3.) Corgi Breed Overview 25
Summary of Pembroke Welsh Corgi Facts.............29
4.) Comparison to the Cardigan Welsh Corgi 31
5.) Corgi Mix Breeds and Types...........................33
Chapter 3 – Things to Think About Before You Buy a Pembroke
Welsh Corgi..36
1.) Do You Need a License?.................................38
2.) How Many Dogs Should You Get?.................39
3.) Do Welsh Corgis Get Along with Other Pets? ..41
4.) Pembroke Welsh Corgi Price and Costs...........42
5.) Pembroke Welsh Corgi Pros and Cons 46
Chapter 4 – Pembroke Welsh Corgi Puppies and Corgi
Puppies for Sale...48
1.) Where Can I Find Corgi Breeders Near Me? 50
2.) How Much are Corgi Puppies? 54
3.) How to Choose a Healthy Welsh Corgi Puppy ..55
4.) Pembroke Welsh Corgi Adoption Information.....57

Chapter 5 – Bringing Your Corgi Home.............................59
  1.) Puppy-Proofing Your Home 60
  2.) What Supplies Do Corgi Puppies Need? 64
  3.) Surviving the First Night with Your Corgi
  Puppy 66
Chapter 6 – Corgi Dog Feeding Guide 68
  1.) Understanding Your Corgi's Nutritional Needs 69
  2.) Tips for Choosing a Healthy Dog Food 72
  3.) Feeding Tips for Corgi Dogs and Puppies........76
Chapter 7 – Corgi Socialization Guide 78
  1.) Creating a Schedule for Your Corgi 79
  2. Socializing Your Corgi Puppy 81
  3.) Play Dates and Puppy Classes 84
Chapter 8 – Corgi Dog Training 86
  1.) Overview of Corgi Training Methods 87
  2.) Best Training Method for the Welsh Corgi.......90
  3.) Corgi House Training Guide...........................92
  4.) Indoor Housetraining for Corgis 94
  5.) Tips for Dealing with Problem Behaviors.........96
Chapter 9 – Corgi Breeding Guide 98
  1.) Things to Think About Before Breeding
  Corgis 99
  2.) Corgi Dog Breeding Information 101
  3.) Tips for Raising Corgi Puppies 104
Chapter 10 – Corgi Health Guide 106
  1.) Common Corgi Health Problems 107
    A. Cataracts 108
    B. Cutaneous Asthenia 108
    C. Cystinuria...109
    D. Degenerative Myelopathy.........................110
    E. Epilepsy..110

F. Hip Dysplasia 111
G. Intervertebral Disk Disease....................... 112
H. Patent Ductus Arteriosus 113
I. Progressive Retinal Atrophy...................... 113
J. Von Willebrand Disease........................... 114
2.) Corgi Vaccinations and Precautions.............. 115
3.) Should You Consider Pet Insurance? 117
Chapter 11 – Corgi Dog Show Guide 119
1.) Pembroke Welsh Corgi Breed Standard.......... 120
A. American Kennel Club Standard.............. 120
B. United Kennel Club Standard.................. 122
C. The Kennel Club (UK) Standard.............. 124
2.) Tips for Showing AKC Corgi Dogs 126
Chapter 12 – Pembroke Welsh Corgi Trusted Resource List 129

CHAPTER 1
Introduction

A t first glance, the Pembroke Welsh Corgi may look a little strange. After all, his legs seem too short for his body and his ears are massive on his head. This small, stubby-legged breed may not look particularly impressive, but if you see him in action you will quickly change your mind. Developed for herding, the Corgi is a bold, intelligent, and active breed – just wait until you see him in action!

The name Corgi actually applies to two separate breeds – the Pembroke Welsh Corgi and the Cardigan Welsh Corgi. Though these two dogs come from the same early breeding stock, they are unique enough to be recognized separately by the American Kennel Club (AKC) and other major breed organizations. Both are some of the smallest herding breeds out there, but their diminutive size doesn't stop them from getting the job done.

Though Corgis were originally bred for herding, their friendly personality and upbeat temperament makes them a great choice for families. Their active and excitable nature sometimes makes them a little tricky to train, but they are highly affectionate, and they love to spend time with family. They are also surprisingly skilled in dog sports like agility and flyball. Simply put, these little dogs have a lot to offer, and they are definitely worthy of your consideration!

Speaking as an experienced Pembroke Welsh Corgi owner, I can say in all honesty that this is one of the best dog breeds I have ever encountered. Not only are these little dogs full of life and love, but they are an absolute joy to have around the house – life is never dull with a Corgi! Choosing to bring home my own Corgi puppy was one of the best decisions I've ever made, and it was the inspiration for me to write this book.

If you've been thinking about getting a Corgi, or if you're simply curious to learn more about the breed, you have come to the right place! In this book you'll learn everything you need to know about the Pembroke Welsh Corgi, including the differences from the Cardigan Welsh Corgi, so you can determine whether this is the right breed for you. We'll cover everything from breed basics to choosing a puppy, preparing your home, and training your new Corgi.

By the time you finish this book, you'll be fully prepared to welcome a Corgi puppy into your home, and you will be eager to do so! I invite you to keep reading now to discover just what makes the Pembroke Welsh Corgi breed so wonderful. Now, let's get started!

Useful Terms to Know

AKC – American Kennel Club, the largest purebred dog registry in the United States

Almond Eye – Referring to an elongated eye shape rather than a rounded shape

Apple Head – A round-shaped skull

Balance – A show term referring to all the parts of the dog, both moving and standing, which produce a harmonious image

Beard – Long, thick hair on the dog's underjaw

Best in Show – An award given to the only undefeated dog left standing at the end of the judging

Bitch – A female dog

Bite – The position of the upper and lower teeth when the dog's jaws are closed; positions include level, undershot, scissors, or overshot

Blaze – A white stripe running down the center of the face between the eyes

Board – To house, feed, and care for a dog for a fee

Breed – A domestic race of dogs having a common gene pool and characterized appearance/function

Breed Standard – A published document describing the look, movement, and behavior of the perfect specimen of a particular breed

Buff – An off-white to gold coloring

Clip – A method of trimming the coat in some breeds

Coat – The hair covering of a dog; some breeds have two coats, and outer coat and undercoat; also known as a double coat. Examples of breeds with double coats include German Shepherd, Siberian Husky, Akita, etc.

Condition – The health of the dog as shown by its skin, coat, behavior, and general appearance

Crate – A container used to house and transport dogs; also called a cage or kennel

Crossbreed (Hybrid) – A dog having a sire and dam of two different breeds; cannot be registered with the AKC

Dam (bitch) – The female parent of a dog

Designer Dog – A dog breed created by crossing two pure breeds.

Dock – To shorten the tail of a dog by surgically removing the end part of the tail.

Double Coat – An outer weather-resistant coat and a soft, waterproof coat for warmth; see above.

Drop Ear – An ear in which the tip of the ear folds over and hangs down; not prick or erect

Entropion – A genetic disorder resulting in the upper or lower eyelid turning in

Fancier – A person who is especially interested in a particular breed or dog sport

Fawn – A red-yellow hue of brown

Feathering – A long fringe of hair on the ears, tail, legs, or body of a dog

Groom – To brush, trim, comb or otherwise make a dog's coat neat in appearance

Heel – To command a dog to stay close to its owner's side

Hip Dysplasia – A condition characterized by the abnormal formation of the hip joint

Inbreeding – The breeding of two closely related dogs of one breed

Kennel – A building or enclosure where dogs are kept

Litter – A group of puppies born at one time

Markings – A contrasting color or pattern on a dog's coat

Mask – Dark shading on the dog's foreface

Mate – To breed a sire and a dam

Neuter – To castrate a male dog or spay a female dog

Pads – The tough, shock-absorbent skin on the bottom of a dog's foot

Parti-Color – A coloration of a dog's coat consisting of two or more definite, well-broken colors; one of the colors must be white

Pedigree – The written record of a dog's genealogy going back three generations or more

Pied – A coloration on a dog consisting of patches of white and another color

Prick Ear – Ear that is carried erect, usually pointed at the tip of the ear

Puppy – A dog under 12 months of age

Purebred – A dog whose sire and dam belong to the same breed and who are of unmixed descent

Saddle – Colored markings in the shape of a saddle over the back; colors may vary

Shedding – The natural process whereby old hair falls off the dog's body as it is replaced by new hair growth

Sire – The male parent of a dog

Smooth Coat – Short hair that is close-lying

Spay – The surgery to remove a female dog's ovaries, rendering her incapable of breeding

Trim – To groom a dog's coat by plucking or clipping

Undercoat – The soft, short coat typically concealed by a longer outer coat

Wean – The process through which puppies transition from subsisting on their mother's milk to eating solid food

Whelping – The act of birthing a litter of puppies

CHAPTER 2
Introduction to the Pembroke Welsh Corgi

S o, you're curious about the Pembroke Welsh Corgi? Then you've come to the right place! In this chapter, you'll receive some basic information about the breed including its history, some interesting facts, and details about the Corgi temperament. You'll also learn more about how the Pembroke Welsh Corgi differs from the Cardigan Welsh Corgi and tidbits about other Corgi mixes. Once you have a firm understanding of the breed, you'll be ready to learn how to care for dogs like Corgis.

1.) Pembroke Welsh Corgi History

As you can probably guess from the name Pembroke Welsh Corgi, this breed was developed in Wales some 1,000 years ago. There are a number of different stories about the breed's origins, some more likely than others. One legend suggests that the dogs were a gift from the fairies who rode them like horses – the legend also says that this is where the saddle pattern on the dog's back comes from. Of course, experts offer a much more likely explanation of the Corgi breed's history.

Though the Corgi doesn't look much like the Siberian Husky, these breeds actually share a similar heritage – they are both descended from northern spitz-type breeds that were brought over to Britain by the Vikings. Other theories suggest that the breed is related to the Norwegian Lundehund and the Swedish Vallhund, or that the early specimens of the breed were brought to Wales during the 12th century by Flemish weavers.

Though the exact origins of the Pembroke Welsh Corgi are up for debate, it is well-known that shepherd's dogs and herding dogs have been around for centuries. Many modern breeds are descendant from dogs that were originally bred and kept by royalty, whereas peasants were often only allowed to keep smaller dogs for the purpose of hunting vermin.

In Britain, the Corgi was used as a general-purpose farm dog, helping to keep poultry from wandering outside the farmyard and controlling vermin. When rearing geese became popular in Wales, Corgis were used to take them to market, driving the geese along the road to town and keeping them in line. The Corgi was perfectly suited to this purpose due to his ability to anticipate moves before they happen and for being quiet so as not to spook the flock. Corgis were also used to herd cattle in some situations, but their skills were better suited for market work.

The modern Pembroke Welsh Corgi first began to gain popularity in Britain during the 1930s when King George VI gifted a Pembroke puppy to his daughters. Even now, Queen Elizabeth II is a fan of the breed. The Pembroke Welsh Corgi and the Cardigan Welsh Corgi were grouped together when they were first shown before The Kennel Club of Britain in 1925, and they were grouped together under the name Welsh Corgi by The Kennel Club in 1928. It wasn't until 1934 that the breeds were recognized as separate and distinct.

The first Pembroke Welsh Corgi was registered with The American Kennel Club in 1934, and the Pembroke Welsh Corgi Club of America (PWCCA) was founded in 1936. The breed continues to enjoy great popularity in the United States, ranking consistently within the top 20 most popular breeds according to AKC registration statistics. Due to a 2007 ban on tail docking, however, the breed has become somewhat rare in the United Kingdom.

2.) Interesting Facts About the Corgi Dog Breed

The Corgi is one of the most easily recognized dog breeds out there. Even if you know nothing about them, you can identify the breed by its short stature, big ears, and a docked tail. These dogs are also well-known for their bright and bubbly personalities. But what else makes the Corgi such a unique and wonderful breed? Here are some interesting facts about the Pembroke Welsh Corgi:

1. The Corgi is a world-class herding dog.

While there are plenty of dog breeds out there that were developed specifically for herding, few are as skilled as the Corgi. Despite their stubby legs, these little dogs can really move, and their bold intelligence helps them excel in the field. Each year, many Pembroke Welsh Corgis compete in AKC herding competitions.

2. Pembroke Welsh Corgis are excellent at dog sports.

Though the breed was developed for herding, his intelligence and agility make him an excellent fit for a wide variety of dog sports. Many Corgis compete in dog sports such as agility, conformation, obedience, flyball, herding, and more. In fact, one Pembroke Welsh Corgi named Belli is a triple champion, the only one of the breed to do so. To earn the title of triple champion, a dog must earn a championship title in both conformation and herding as well as a title in agility, obedience, or tracking.

3. The name Corgi means "dwarf dog."

Though the exact origins of the Corgi and its name are hard to determine, many dog experts believe that that breed's name is a description of the dog in Welsh. The Welsh word "cor" means to watch over or gather while the suffix "gi" is a form of the Welsh word meaning dog. Others say that the word "cor" means dwarf which, combined with the Welsh word "gi" for dog, translates to dwarf dog.

4. Some Pembroke Welsh Corgis are born without tails.

Tail docking is the practice of removing a portion of a dog's tail, and it is a practice that has been banned in many countries. Centuries ago, tail docking was thought to prevent rabies, though it also helped to prevent injuries in breeds used for fighting and baiting. In fact, tail docking is a standard requirement for some AKC breeds. Early Corgis had their tails docked to distinguish the dogs kept by peasants from those kept by royalty to prevent the poaching of royal game. The practice continued for many years, and a long history of tail docking has led to some Corgis being born without tails.

5. Corgis make excellent watchdogs.

As a herding breed, the Corgi has a naturally watchful and attentive nature. He is by no means inherently aggressive, but he will bark to alert you to the presence of a stranger on the property – even if it is only a squirrel.

6. Pembroke Welsh Corgis have a double coat.

As is typical for dogs descended from spitz-type breeds, the Corgi has a double coat. These dogs have a soft, dense undercoat that protects them from the cold with a longer topcoat. The length of the dog's coat varies on different parts of the body, though it should never be too long or have excessive feathering. Corgis shed continuously throughout the year but "blow" their coat at least twice, typically in the fall and spring.

7. The Corgi breed comes in a wide variety of colors.

When you picture the Pembroke Welsh Corgi, you probably think of him with a red and white coat. In reality, this breed comes in a wide variety of different colors, though the pattern of markings is fairly standard across the breed. There are 5 basic colors for the Pembroke Welsh Corgi, most accompanied by white trim with a saddle pattern on the back and a mask across the face.

8. Corgis love to eat.

Sure, all dogs love to eat, but the Corgi is known for having a bottomless pit for a stomach. This usually isn't a problem, as long as your Corgi gets plenty of exercise to work off his energy, but you should still monitor his intake. Your Corgi may not grow any taller, but he can certainly grow wider, and obesity is just as dangerous for dogs as it is for humans – make sure you feed your dog healthy dog food and don't give him too many table scraps.

9. The Corgi is very fond of children.

Though Pembroke Welsh Corgis love people of all ages, they have a special affinity for children. You should be mindful, however, of the fact that his herding nature may make your Corgi prone to nipping at a child's feet or ankles. Because these dogs are so smart and quick to learn, however, you can train them against this behavior from a young age.

10. The Corgi's shortness is caused by a genetic mutation.

While many dog breeds have been bred down in size of the years (like the Miniature Poodle), the Corgi's short stature is actually caused by a genetic mutation. Chondrodysplasia, also known as canine dwarfism, causes the abnormal development of bones and cartilage – short limbs are the primary distinguishing characteristic of a dog with chondrodysplasia.

3.) Corgi Breed Overview

When you see the Pembroke Welsh Corgi for the first time, you will undoubtedly notice his short legs and his thick coat. If you take the time to get to know him, however, you will find that the Corgi temperament is incredibly unique and wonderful. Not only are these dogs skilled in herding and dog sports, but they make excellent family pets, especially for families. If you are looking for a fun and friendly little dog who will win your heart from the moment you set eyes on him, the Corgi may just be the breed for you.

Before you decide if the Corgi is the dog of your dreams, take the time to learn as much as you can about him. Technically speaking, there are two distinct Corgi breeds – the Pembroke Welsh Corgi and the Cardigan Welsh Corgi. We'll talk more about the differences in the next chapter but, for now, let's focus on the Pembroke Corgi.

The Pembroke Welsh Corgi is a smaller dog, but he walks the line between being a small-breed and a medium-breed dog. Most Corgis reach 25 to 30 pounds (11.3 to 13.6 kg) at maturity and stand somewhere between 10 and 12 inches (25.4 to 30.5 cm) tall. This breed is recognized by the American Kennel Club and categorized in the Herding group. In fact, he is the smallest member of that group. The Kennel Club places him in the Pastoral Group and the FCI in Group 1 as a Sheepdog.

Developed specifically for herding, Corgi breeds are very intelligent and hardworking. They have the ability to work independently, which can sometimes give them a bit of a stubborn streak. However, these dogs learn quickly, and they respond well to positive reinforcement, so any stubbornness can be controlled with firm and consistent obedience training. These dogs also do very well in dog sports such as agility, conformation, obedience, and flyball.

The typical Corgi personality is bright and friendly – these little dogs form close attachments to family and can be very affectionate by nature. Though developed as a working breed, modern Corgis make wonderful family pets, and many of them have an affinity for children. Due to their herding nature, however, you may find that your dog sometimes tries to herd your children by nipping at their heels – this behavior should be curbed early with obedience training and interactions with young children should always be supervised.

Another wonderful feature of the Pembroke Welsh Corgi personality is his goofy nature. These dogs do tend to get into mischief, but mostly in non-destructive ways. Your Corgi will invent his own games and find new ways to amuse himself, so you need to maintain a firm and consistent hand in leadership to dissuade undesirable behaviors as soon as they start. If you let your dog get away with something once, it will be that much harder to dissuade him from doing it again.

Dogs like Corgis respond well to training, and they have a natural desire to learn. To counteract your dog's independent nature and high energy levels, however, you'll have to start training him as early as possible and be consistent with your commands. Once you choose a command, stick with it and be consistent about enforcing house rules. There is never a need to be harsh with a Corgi, but you should be firm and establish yourself as the authority figure in the household.

In addition to basic obedience training, you'll have to work with your Corgi to control his voice because many Corgis develop an affinity for barking. This habit can be helpful if you want your dog to be a watchdog, but it can become annoying if he does it all the time. Corgis are capable of learning from a very young age, and they will soak up everything you have to teach them, so start early!

Generally speaking, Corgis get along fairly well with other dogs, and they can be compatible with cats and other household pets as well. You should always supervise early interactions between your dog and other animals until you know how he will respond. The same is true for children and for strangers. This breed can sometimes be wary of unfamiliar people, but he will warm up quickly and respond to cues from his owner.

While the Pembroke Welsh Corgi's short legs are his primary distinguishing feature, there are other physical characteristics that make him unique as well. As a descendant of spitz-type dogs, the Corgi has a thick double coat, a fox-like face, and large pointed ears. The typical Corgi coat consists of a dense, fine undercoat and a medium-length topcoat. These dogs shed consistently throughout the year but caring for the coat is fairly simple – just brush it as often as you can and keep in mind that your dog will shed more heavily during the spring and fall.

When it comes to Corgi coat colors, the most common include red, sable, black, and fawn. Most dogs of this breed have white markings, and tricolor Pembroke Welsh Corgis are fairly common as well. Most dogs of this breed have a "fairy saddle" on their back which, according to legend, exists because Corgis were the dog of choice for fairies who rode them like horses. However, In reality, this marking is caused by a change in the thickness and direction of that portion of the dog's coat.

Another unique feature of the breed is the Corgi tail, though perhaps it would be more accurately described as the Corgi lack-of-tail. In the early years of the breed, the tail was docked very short. Now, modern breeders often continue to dock the breed's tail, though it is also possible for Corgis to be born with a very short tail or virtually no tail at all. Another interesting point to be made about Corgi genetics is the fact that their short stature is an inherited trait linked to a condition known as chondrodysplasia – you already learned about that in the previous section.

Aside from his chondrodysplasia, Pembroke Welsh Corgi dogs are generally a healthy breed. However, there is a risk for certain inherited conditions such as hip dysplasia, epilepsy, patent ductus arteriosus, and von Willebrand disease. Other conditions to which the breed may be prone include cataracts, cutaneous asthenia, cystinuria, degenerative myelopathy, intervertebral disk disease, retinal dysplasia, and progressive retinal atrophy. The average lifespan of the breed is 12 to 14 years.

Summary of Pembroke Welsh Corgi Facts

Pedigree: descended from spitz-type breeds, perhaps with influence from the Norwegian Lundehund and the Swedish Vallhund

AKC Group: Herding Group

Kennel Club Group (UK): Pastoral Group

FCI Group: Group 1, Section 1, Sheepdogs

Breed Size: small to medium

Height: 10 to 12 inches (25.4 to 30.5 cm)

Weight: 25 to 30 pounds (11.3 to 13.6 kg)

Coat Length: short undercoat, medium-length topcoat

Coat Texture: fine, dense undercoat;

Color: red, sable, black fawn, tricolor; often with white markings

Eyes and Nose: dark brown

Ears: large and pointed

Tail: short; docked or non-existent

Temperament: active, friendly, bold, goofy

Strangers: may be wary of strangers, likely to bark

Other Dogs: generally good with other dogs

Other Pets: generally, gets along with other pets

Training: intelligent and very trainable; may develop a stubborn streak; requires firm and consistent training

Exercise Needs: very active and energetic

Health Conditions: hip dysplasia, epilepsy, patent ductus arteriosus, von Willebrand disease, cataracts, cutaneous asthenia, cystinuria, degenerative myelopathy, intervertebral disk disease, retinal dysplasia, and progressive retinal atrophy

Lifespan: average 12 to 14 years

4.) Comparison to the Cardigan Welsh Corgi

For years, the Pembroke Welsh Corgi and Cardigan Welsh Corgi were shown together under the name Welsh Corgi. It wasn't until 1934 that the breeds were recognized as separate and distinct. What you need to know is that the two breeds are still very similar. However, there are some subtle differences in both the physical appearance and temperament traits for the two breeds.

Both the Pembroke Welsh Corgi and the Cardigan Welsh Corgi were developed in Wales and used for both herding and vermin control. Having descended from spitz-type dogs, both breeds have a foxlike appearance with a double coat. One of the biggest physical differences between the two is that the Pembroke's tail is traditionally docked, while the Cardigan's is not.

Aside from the major Corgi tail difference, there are some other points of differentiation between the two breeds. The Cardigan Corgi, for example, is a little heavier than the Pembroke – he reaches an average weight of 25 to 38 pounds (11.3 to 17.2 kg) and a height of 10.5 to 12.5 inches (26.7 to 31.75 cm). Pembroke Corgis also have more oval-shaped feet that, on the front legs, remain straight or turn slightly inward. The Cardigan's feet are more rounded, and the front feet tend to curve outward.

There are also subtle differences in coloration between the two Corgi breeds. Both breeds may exhibit different shades of red, sable, fawn, or black with white markings, but the Cardigan is also likely to exhibit blue merle or brindle colorations. Most Cardigan Welsh Corgis also have white markings on the neck and chest as well as the feet and the tip of the tail. For the more common colorations, however, you may not be able to tell the difference between the two breeds based on coat alone.

Both Corgi breeds are active and intelligent, they love to herd, and they can be very affectionate with family. Both breeds are naturally somewhat suspicious of strangers, which makes early socialization and training essential. Some owners of the breed suggest that the Pembroke Corgi is more affectionate and even-tempered than the Cardigan Corgi, but both of these breeds can be influenced by socialization and interaction. Cardigan Welsh Corgis may make better watchdogs, though both breeds tend to bark at strangers and animals in the yard.

5.) Corgi Mix Breeds and Types

You've probably heard the term "designer dog" thrown around, but what does it actually mean? A designer dog is little more than a mixed breed or, to put it another way, a mutt. Mixed breed dogs have existed for as long as dogs themselves and accidental crossings were the foundation for numerous modern breeds. Even so, many dog owners today like the idea of crossing two of their favorite breeds to create what they consider the ideal dog.

Technically speaking, it is possible to cross just about any breed with any other. There are some logistics to consider in terms of size, however, especially in cases where a male dog of a large breed is bred to a female dog of a small breed – it can be dangerous for small dogs to carry large puppies. You also have to consider the health problems to which either breed is prone. If you breed two dogs, who are carriers for a genetic condition, the risk that the puppies will inherit it is very high.

So, why would anyone want to breed a Pembroke Welsh Corgi to another breed? There are many potential reasons, though most of them are cosmetic. For example, if you wanted a Corgi with a curly coat, you might breed him with a Miniature Poodle. If you wanted a Corgi to be smaller than the breed average, you might breed him to a toy breed like a Pomeranian or a Chihuahua.

Another reason for Corgi mix dogs is to create some kind of unique color combination or pattern. Pembroke Welsh Corgi colors already include red, sable, fawn, black and tan. There are also tricolor corgis, though depending on the other breed you use in the mix, you could create a tricolor corgi with colors outside the standard corgi colors. You could also create a blue merle corgi, a black corgi, a black and white corgi, or even a white corgi, though some Pembroke Welsh Corgis are white – it just isn't a color preferred for showing.

Since we're on the subject of Pembroke Welsh Corgi mixed breeds, let's take a minute to talk about some of the most common Corgi mix puppies you might encounter. Here are some common crossings:

- German Shephergi (Corgi Shepherd mix)
- Labragi (Corgi Labrador mix)
- Corgherd (Corgi Australian Shepherd mix)
- Husgi (Siberian Husky Corgi mix)
- Beagi (Beagle Corgi mix)
- Shigi (Shiba Inu Corgi mix)
- Cohuahua (Corgi Chihuahua mix)
- Cattlegi (Cattle Dog Corgi mix)
- Corgiever (Corgi Golden Retriever mix)
- Rottgi (Rottweiler Corgi mix)
- Corrier (Corgi Terrier mix)
- Pitgi (Pitbull Corgi mix)

In addition to different corgi mix breeds, you may also come across Corgis of nonstandard size. Some breeders offer what they call Teacup Corgis or Miniature Corgis. Be very careful about buying one of these dogs. The Corgi is already a fairly small dog, so if you find a breeder offering a Teacup Corgi or Mini Corgi, be sure to ask how they accomplished the smaller size. It may simply be that they bred two smaller Corgis together or they may have bred a small Pembroke Welsh Corgi to a different toy breed. It is important to know the difference, because improper breeding practices can put your puppy at risk for musculoskeletal issues later in life.

CHAPTER 3
Things to Think About Before You Buy a Pembroke Welsh Corgi

Now that you know a little more about the Pembroke Welsh Corgi breed, you may have a better idea whether it is the right breed for you or not. Before you make your final decision, however, I encourage you to think about some of the more practical aspects of owning a Corgi. In this chapter, we'll talk about things like licensing your dog and introducing your Corgi to other pets. You'll also receive an estimation and breakdown of costs for keeping Corgis, as well as a list of pros and cons for the breed.

1.) Do You Need a License?

Dogs are far and away the most commonly kept pet, so most people don't consider that there might be legal requirements for keeping one. Though these requirements vary, most states in the United States require dog owners to license their dogs after the age of six months. A dog license in the U.S. usually only costs about $25 (£22.50), and you can renew it annually as long as you have proof that your dog has been vaccinated against rabies. In some states, you may even be able to purchase a lifetime license.

As is true for many things, dog licensing requirements in the UK are different from the U.S. While the U.S. has no federal requirements for dog licensing, the UK makes it mandatory for all dogs to be licensed. The cost for a dog license is similar, though there is no requirement that a dog be vaccinated for rabies because rabies has been completely eradicated from the UK.

In addition to determining whether you need a license for your Pembroke Welsh Corgi, you should also look into other requirements that might come up. For example, some apartment buildings have rules against keeping pets like dogs, or you might have to pay an additional deposit or monthly fee. There may also be requirements for traveling with your dog. For example, anyone bringing an animal into or out of the UK is required to have an Animal Movement License (AML), and the animal may be subjected to a quarantine period on either end of the trip.

2.) How Many Dogs Should You Get?

If you love dogs, you might be thinking about getting more than one Pembroke Welsh Corgi. I don't blame you – the only thing better than one Corgi is two of them! Before you go and get a handful of puppies, however, I recommend that you take your time to think about the practical aspects of this decision. First, do Pembroke Welsh Corgis get along with other dogs? Second, can you care for more than one dog? Third, are you able to afford more than one dog?

To answer the first question, Pembroke Welsh Corgis are generally good with other dogs. As a herding breed, however, they were developed to work independently, so the Corgi is not naturally the most dog-loving breed. Many Corgi owners will tell you that the breed can sometimes be a bit pushy toward other dogs and individual temperaments vary. However, if you are able to raise the puppies together, and you commit to early training and socialization, you shouldn't have a problem.

To address the other two questions, you'll have to answer these for yourself. As you'll learn through reading this book, Pembroke Welsh Corgis are definitely not one of the more high-maintenance breeds, but all dogs require a certain amount of time and care. Fortunately, many of the most time-consuming aspects of caring for a dog are easy to multiply. You can feed and walk both dogs at the same time, and you can take them to the vet together. You may need to separate them for training, but most aspects of dog care are just as easy to do for two dogs, as for one.

What you'll really need to think about before bringing home two Corgi puppies instead of one is whether you can cover the financial burden. You'll have to buy twice as much dog food, pay for twice as many vet visits, and cover twice the boarding or pet-sitting costs if you go out of town. You might get lucky and have two Corgis who never get sick, or you could end up with two dogs who have serious health problems. There is no way to predict what will happen, so make sure you are able to cover the cost if something should arise before you commit to two dogs.

3.) Do Welsh Corgis Get Along with Other Pets?

In addition to considering whether your Pembroke Welsh Corgi might do well with a second dog, you need to think about how well he is going to get along with your other pets – if you have them. For the most part, Corgis get along with cats – at least with cats they know. In the same way that a Corgi might become shy or pushy with an unfamiliar dog, the same can be true for unfamiliar cats. As long as you raise your Corgi puppy with pets, however, everything should be fine.

Whether your Corgi is used to cats and other pets or not, you should always supervise interactions. When you bring your Corgi puppy home for the first time, you don't know how he is going to react to anything. Plus, as much as you may know the pets you already have, animals can be unpredictable. Make any introductions slowly and carefully to avoid problems, and don't leave your Corgi and your other pets alone until you know how they are going to act around each other.

4.) Pembroke Welsh Corgi Price and Costs

Before you decide to bring home a Pembroke Welsh Corgi, you should have a good idea what kind of costs you are looking at. Don't just consider the initial costs for your puppy and for the necessary supplies – make sure that you can handle the recurring monthly and annual costs as well!

When it comes to the initial costs for a Pembroke Welsh Corgi, you have to think about the cost to purchase a puppy as well as the basic supplies like food and water bowls, grooming supplies, cleaning supplies, a crate and bed, plus plenty of toys. You'll also want to factor in the cost of early vaccinations, spay/neuter surgery, microchipping and licensing your dog.

Pembroke Welsh Corgi puppies usually cost between $600 and $1,000 (£430 - £718), though puppies bred for show may cost as much as $2,000 (£1,435). The cost for basic supplies including food and water dishes, grooming supplies, and cleaning supplies should be under $100 (£72) and you can purchase a small crate and dog bed for about $50 (£36). The cost for toys will vary depending which ones you choose and how many you buy, but you should be able to get a decent assortment for less than $50 (£36).

As for the additional upfront costs, those costs will vary depending on where you go. You can save a lot of money by finding a local vet clinic where you can get your Pembroke Welsh Corgi's initial vaccinations for under $50 (£36) per visit, or about $200 (£144) total for four rounds. Microchipping is not required in the USA but is highly recommended and usually costs about

$30 (£22). The cost to have your dog licensed is similar. Spay and neuter surgery can be very costly if you go to a regular vet, but you will probably pay about $100 (£72) for spay surgery and $50 (£36) for neuter surgery, at a local clinic or rescue.

To give you a visual representation of these initial costs for keeping a Pembroke Welsh Corgi, here is a breakdown in chart form for one and two dogs:

Initial Costs for Pembroke Welsh Corgis		
Cost	One Dog	Two Dogs
Pembroke Welsh Corgi Puppy Cost	$600 to $2,000 (£430 to £1,435)	$1,200 to $4,000 (£861 - £2,871)
Basic Supplies	$100 (£72)	$100 (£72)
Crate and Dog Bed	$50 (£36)	$100 (£72)
Assortment of Toys	$50 (£36)	$100 (£72)
Vaccinations	$200 (£144)	$400 (£288)
Microchipping	$30 (£22)	$60 (£44)
Dog License	$30 (£22)	$60 (£44)
Spay or Neuter Surgery (Clinic)	$50 to $100 (£36 to £72)	$100 to $200 (£72 to £144)
Total	$1,110 to $2,560 (£790 to £1837)	$2,120 to $5,020 (£1,522 to £3,603)

In addition to paying for the upfront costs of keeping a Pembroke Welsh Corgi, there are certain costs you'll have to cover on a monthly or annual basis as well. These costs include food and treats, grooming, veterinary care, and replacements for toys and supplies.

As a small-breed dog, your Pembroke Welsh Corgi may not eat as much as larger dogs. Keep in mind, however, that they are a working breed, so they need a calorie-dense diet designed to support the fast metabolism of smaller, hardworking dogs. You can buy a large bag of dog food that will last about a month for under $40 (£29). Add to that the cost of a couple bags of treats per month and you have a monthly cost around $60 (£43).

For the remaining costs, you won't need to cover these things every month, but you should keep them in mind. You'll need to take your Corgi to the vet about twice a year, and each visit will cost about $45 (£32). If you divide the cost of two visits over twelve months, you should be setting aside about $7.50 (£4.30) per month. Grooming is also something you may only need to do a few times a year, so set aside about $10 (£7.20) a month for this cost. Finally, budget about $10 (£7.20) per month for replacement toys and supplies.

To give you a visual representation of these monthly costs for keeping a Pembroke Welsh Corgi, here is a breakdown in chart form for one and two dogs:

Monthly Costs for Pembroke Welsh Corgis		
Cost	One Dog	Two Dogs
Food and Treats	$60 (£43)	$120 (£86)
Veterinary Costs	$7.50 (£4.30)	$15 (£11)
Grooming	$10 (£7.20)	$20 (£14)
Replacements	$10 (£7.20)	$20 (£14)
Total	$87.50 (£63)	$175 (£126)

5.) Pembroke Welsh Corgi Pros and Cons

By now you should have a pretty good idea what it is like to keep a Pembroke Welsh Corgi as a pet. Bringing home a new puppy is a big decision, however, so you need to think about it from all angles – that means considering the pros as well as the cons. To help you out, here is a list of pros and cons about the Pembroke Welsh Corgi breed:

Pros for the Pembroke Corgi:

- Corgis are a fairly small breed, so they may be easier to handle than larger dogs.
- Most Corgis are adaptable to different living situations as long as their needs for exercise are met.
- Although the Corgi has a thick double coat, brushing it is fairly straightforward, and professional grooming or trimming is not usually necessary.
- The Corgi is an intelligent dog that responds well to training when properly motivated.
- Corgis learn quickly, and they can excel in a variety of different dog sports.
- The Corgi is generally good with children, especially when raised with them.
- Corgis are affectionate with family, and they are generally very good with people.
- The Corgi makes a good watchdog because he will bark at strangers.

- Corgis are fun-loving and entertaining to keep as pets – they will keep you on your toes.

Cons for the Pembroke Corgi:

- The Corgi's herding instincts may cause him to nip at children or try to herd other pets.
- Corgis tend to bark a lot, though this behavior can be curbed with training.
- The Corgi is a working breed and thus has a very high need for exercise.
- Because the Corgi is an intelligent breed, he requires significant mental stimulation, in addition to exercise.
- The Corgi's compressed structure puts him at risk for certain musculoskeletal issues.
- Corgis are prone to a number of serious health problems including inherited conditions – this means that responsible breeding is very important.
- The Corgi's coat sheds moderately throughout the year and heavily twice a year, spring and fall.

CHAPTER 4
Pembroke Welsh Corgi Puppies and Corgi Puppies for Sale

H opefully, by now, you have a thorough understanding of the Pembroke Welsh Corgi breed, and what makes it so great. You should also know the basics of what to expect when you become a Corgi owner. The next step, then, is to think about where you are going to get your puppy, or whether you should consider adopting an adult dog instead. In this chapter, we'll talk about where to find Corgi breeders, how much to pay for a puppy, and how to choose a healthy puppy from a litter. We'll also cover Pembroke Welsh Corgi adoption information.

1.) Where Can I Find Corgi Breeders Near Me?

When you're ready to start thinking about getting a Pembroke Welsh Corgi of your own, you need to consider where you're going to look for Corgi puppies for sale. Your first instinct might be to head to your local pet shop to see if they have any corgi puppies. While this is certainly an option, you should think twice before you buy a puppy from a pet store. Unfortunately, many pet stores get their puppies from puppy mills which means that the puppy you bring home is likely poorly bred and may be at risk for major health problems down the line.

Instead of going to a pet store, your first step should be to locate some Corgi puppy breeders in your area. Purchasing a puppy from a breeder is a much better idea than buying from a pet store because a breeder is more likely to have carefully selected his breeding stock, and should have tested for inherited health problems, to avoid passing them on. The puppies themselves are also more likely to have been socialized from a young age, which is important.

So, if you're wondering "Where can I find Corgi puppies near me?" you should start asking around. Check with your local vet's office, to see if anyone has connections to a local breeder. If there are no Pembroke Welsh Corgi breeders in your immediate area, you might need to expand the search.

Try an online search, and you might find some helpful resources. For example, the American Kennel Club has a breeder's directory that allows you to search by breed – this is a great option to find breeders that may have Pembroke Welsh Corgi puppies for sale. You can also try the Pembroke Welsh Corgi Club of America, or simply do a search using the terms, "Corgi puppies for sale near me."

Now, don't go and put down a deposit with the first breeder you come across who has a Pembroke Welsh Corgi puppy for sale. Once you've done the research to find Corgi breeders, you need to go through that list again and narrow down your options, to find the best one. Start by removing from the list breeders who offer both Pembroke and Cardigan Welsh Corgi puppies. If you are going to buy a Corgi puppy, you want to make sure that the breeder you choose is dedicated to and experienced with the breed.

Your next step is to do a little more research on the different breeders, and then actually contact them to determine whether they're a legitimate operation or not. Here are some simple steps to take:

1. View the website for each breeder and evaluate the information provided. Ask yourself:
   - Does the website look professional?
   - Does the breeder offer credentials, certifications, and AKC membership info?
   - Are there pictures of the breeding stock?
   - Is there proof of DNA testing and responsible breeding?
   - Are there any red flags such as exorbitant prices, or a lack of information?

2. Remove from your list any breeders that don't provide adequate information for you to determine whether they are a legitimate operation and not just a hobby breeder.

3. Contact the remaining breeders on your list and ask them some questions:
   - What made you choose the Pembroke Welsh Corgi breed?
   - How did you get started with breeding, and why?
   - How much experience do you have breeding Corgis?

- How do you ensure the health of your breeding stock and their puppies?
- Are you willing to provide proof of AKC registration and DNA testing?
- What is your policy for reserving a puppy?

4. After talking to the breeders, you should be able to narrow your list further to one or two options. At that point, you should visit the breeder to complete your search.

5. When you visit the breeder, ask for a tour of the facilities and make sure you see everything, including:
   - The breeding stock (to determine that they are of the right breed, and in good health).
   - The puppies (to make sure they are healthy and active).
   - The facilities (to make sure they are clean and well-maintained).
   - Testimonials from previous buyers.

At this point, you should know whether the breeder is trustworthy and experienced enough for you to buy a puppy from them. Determine what the policy is to put down a deposit, and then you can move to the next step – picking your Pembroke Welsh Corgi puppy from the litter.

2.) How Much Are Corgi Puppies?

As you start looking around for a Corgi dog for sale, you should ask yourself, "How much are Corgis?" The answer to this question is not simple, unfortunately, because many factors go into determining a fair Corgi puppy cost. First and foremost, a purebred Pembroke Welsh Corgi is going to cost more than a mixed breed or simply a puppy that wasn't bred from an AKC-registered sire or dam. You'll find Corgis for sale that are not AKC-registered, and you certainly have the option to purchase one, just be aware that you may not be able to show your dog if you can't prove that he is purebred and from AKC stock.

When it comes to Corgi puppies, the price can vary greatly. Generally speaking, the minimum Corgi puppy cost is about $600 (£425). The range for puppies is usually between $600 and $1,000 (£425 to £709), though you can certainly find Corgi puppies for sale with a price tag as high as $2,000 (£1,418). Just ask yourself what your priorities are to determine your ideal Corgi puppy price. If you want to breed and show your dog, go for a purebred AKC-registered puppy and pay the higher price tag. If you're just looking for a pet, these things may not be necessary, and you can pay a lower price.

While you are looking for breeders, you may come across breeders who have Corgi mix puppies for sale. Mixed breeds have started to become popular, and many breeders sell them as "designer dogs." It is completely up to you whether you choose a purebred Pembroke Welsh Corgi or a mix but be aware that even if they are marketed as designer dogs, Corgi mix puppies are just that – mixed breeds. You should not pay the same Corgi dog price for a mixed breed, as for a purebred.

3.) How to Choose a Healthy Welsh Corgi Puppy

Once you've done the work to narrow down your list of breeders, next comes the fun part – picking out your baby Corgi! There is nothing more adorable than a cute, fluffy Corgi puppy. But, you need to keep a level head and avoid getting caught up in the excitement. Bringing home a new puppy is a big responsibility, so you need to make sure that you do it right!

So, when you're at the breeder and ready to pick out your puppy from an available litter of Welsh Corgi puppies, what do you do? Here are some tips:

- Start by observing the puppies to see how they interact with each other – make sure they are playful and energetic, not lethargic or depressed.
- Approach the puppies but don't interact yet – wait and see if they come to you then see how they respond.
- If the puppies are interested in you, you can start to interact and play with them a bit – just be gentle!
- Take a few minutes to interact with each puppy to gauge his temperament to see if he might be a good fit.
- Narrow down your options to a few of the Pembroke Welsh Corgi puppies and give them a closer inspection.
- Check the puppies for obvious signs of illness or injury – look for things such as the following:
    o Clear, bright eyes with no signs of discharge.
    o Clean ears – no redness, swelling, or odor.
    o No sign of diarrhea (dirty under the tail).

- o Clean and soft fur with no patches missing
- o No bumps or visible wounds on the body.
- o Healthy activity and sound movement.

If you're able to determine that the puppy is healthy, and his personality is a good match, talk to the breeder about putting down a deposit. A responsible breeder won't send you home with a puppy who isn't fully weaned, or one under the age of 8 weeks.

4.) Pembroke Welsh Corgi Adoption Information

Buying a Corgi puppy from a breeder is not your only option. Having a puppy is great, but it isn't the right choice for everyone. After all, raising a puppy takes a lot of time and work, so if you're not up to the task, you might want to think about a different option – Corgi adoption.

Every year, millions of pets enter the shelter system, and many of them never make it out. There are plenty of people out there who believe that adoption is always the better option – that no one should purchase a puppy from a breeder. While you are free to make up your own mind on that point, it is worth discussing the pros and cons of Corgi rescue, before you settle your mind.

Corgi puppies are amazing, but they can be quite a handful. Adopting an adult dog from a shelter is just as much a responsibility, but it may not be quite so much work as raising, socializing, and training a new puppy. If you were to adopt from a Corgi dog rescue, you might find that an adult dog is already housetrained, already spayed or neutered, and may also have some obedience training already under his belt. Plus, adult dogs are already fairly set in their personalities, so you can tell through interaction whether the dog is a good fit.

Another benefit of Welsh Corgi adoption is that you'll save money! Rather than spending hundreds of dollars on a puppy, you'll pay an adoption fee in the range of $100 to $150. You'll also have peace of mind knowing that you are saving a life and contributing to a good cause. Pembroke Welsh Corgi adoption is a wonderful thing!

Something you should know if you're considering adoption is that you may have to look a little harder and wait a little longer if you have your heart set on a puppy. While puppies do come through the system, adult dogs are more common. Try contacting your local shelter to see if they have any Corgi puppies for adoption or do an online search for a dedicated Corgi rescue. You can also just try searching with the terms, "Corgis for adoption near me."

CHAPTER 5

Bringing Your Corgi Home

N ow that you know everything you need to know about finding a Corgi puppy or adopting from a shelter, you're probably eager to bring your own Corgi home! However, before you take that step, you need to make some preparations. In this chapter, we'll cover the basics about puppy-proofing your home, and for purchasing all of the necessary supplies for your new puppy. You'll also receive some helpful advice for surviving the first night at home with your new Corgi puppy.

1.) Puppy-Proofing Your Home

Puppy-proofing your home is as much about keeping your home and your belongings in good shape as it is keeping your puppy protected from harm. You might think that puppy-proofing is as simple as just picking a few things up off the floor, but it is much more in-depth than that. At least, it should be. Here are some of the different parts of your home you should look at when it comes time to puppy-proof things:

- Your kitchen and pantry
- All bathrooms
- Bedrooms and guest rooms
- Living room and other living spaces
- Dining room
- Laundry room
- Garage and shed
- Front yard and back yard
- Gardens and beds

That's right! You need to look at every part of your home, inside and out, to make sure there is nothing that could potentially harm your puppy. Even if you think a room is clean and safe, it couldn't hurt to take a second look. Puppies are naturally inquisitive, and they will put anything in their mouths; don't make the mistake of leaving something where your puppy could find it!

Okay, so how do you go about puppy-proofing your home? The first step is to put yourself in your puppy's shoes and take a good hard look at your home, inside and out, to identify any potential hazards or things that might be appealing to a curious pup. Next, address those hazards by putting them somewhere out of reach or by making sure your puppy won't be able to access that area. Finally, keep it up! You'll need to puppy-proof your entire house and yard up front, but you'll also need to keep up with your puppy-proofing strategies to keep your Corgi safe.

Though you'll need to go through your entire house on your own, here are some major points to hit when it comes time for puppy-proofing:

- Make sure all the doors and windows in your home close securely.
- If you have pet doors, make sure they are the right size and ensure that you can close and lock them, if needed.
- Put away all food in the kitchen and pantry; don't leave anything out on the counter.
- Make sure that food containers are secure; they shouldn't spill if they are knocked over.
- Keep dangerous foods to dogs, like chocolate and onions, well out of reach.
- Keep your cleaning supplies in a locked cabinet, or on a shelf, your puppy can't reach.
- Make sure your drawers and cabinet doors are not easy for your puppy to open.

- Secure your trash in a lidded container or place it in a cabinet with a childproof lock.
- Make sure plastic bags are not somewhere your puppy can reach.
- Keep all medications and toiletries in the medicine cabinet or in drawers where your puppy can't get to them.
- Keep the lid on the toilet bowl closed just in case your puppy gets up on the toilet.
- Put cat food and litter boxes somewhere your puppy won't be able to access them.
- Put away all toys and small objects. Nothing that can fit in your puppy's mouth should be left on the floor or within reach.
- Check to see whether your houseplants are poisonous. If they are, get rid of them or put them out of reach.
- Outside: make sure that all lawn care products are securely put away.
- Don't leave tools like rakes and shovels unsecured.
- Keep your garbage cans tightly covered and properly dispose of all trash and recyclables including yard waste.
- Check to see whether any of your garden plants are poisonous – if so, get rid of them, or fence them in.
- Cover any open bodies of water like ponds, pools, or water features.
- Make sure that your garage door shuts completely, so your puppy can't get into it.

Even though you are going to take these steps to puppy-proof your home, you should still take basic precautions. Always supervise your puppy when he is not contained – this means keeping him in the same room as you, at all times! You should also make sure he has a wide selection of chew toys to keep him busy, so he doesn't look for other things, (potentially dangerous things), to chew on. And, adopt an attitude of "better safe than sorry." If you aren't sure whether something is safe for your puppy, it is better to presume that it isn't!

2.) What Supplies Do Corgi Puppies Need?

Generally speaking, Pembroke Welsh Corgis are not high-maintenance dogs. That said, you are definitely going to need a few supplies before you bring your Corgi puppy home for the first time. Here's a quick list of things you'll need, for starters, for proper corgi care:

- A crate
- A crate mat or dog bed
- A puppy playpen
- Food and water bowls
- Assortment of toys
- Grooming supplies
- Cleaning supplies

In addition to these supplies, you'll also need puppy food and treats – we'll talk more about those in the next chapter. For now, however, let's take a closer look at the supplies on the list above.

First and foremost, you'll need a crate to keep your Pembroke Corgi puppy contained overnight and when you can't physically supervise him yourself. Your Corgi puppy is going to be pretty small when you bring him home, so you should choose a small crate – ideally one just large enough for him to comfortably lie down and turn around in. You might be able to get away with a crate large enough to contain your Corgi when he is full-grown if you don't want to spend the money buying a separate puppy crate. You might also want to consider a wire crate that comes with a divider, so you can make it smaller for your puppy and remove the divider, as he grows.

To make your puppy's crate comfortable, purchase a crate mat or dog bed. Keep in mind that your puppy might have accidents in the crate, so don't spend a whole lot of money – you might even just want to use an old blanket or towel for the first couple of weeks. It's also a good idea to purchase a puppy playpen – something made of lightweight metal mesh or wire that you can easily move around the house. You can use the playpen to keep your puppy contained in rooms that don't have doors or to simply create a space for your puppy to call his own.

In terms of additional supplies, you'll need the basics like food and water bowls, grooming supplies, and cleaning supplies. For food and water bowls, stainless steel is a good option because it is easy to clean. If your puppy is a voracious eater, however, he might end up tipping the bowls over – something a little heavier like ceramic might be a better choice, at first. For grooming supplies, a wire pin brush and an undercoat rake are good for starters and be sure to invest in a high-quality, natural stain remover.

For toys, you'll want to purchase a variety at first, and then see which ones your Corgi puppy likes best. You'll want a couple of plush toys for your puppy to sleep with, and a few chew toys – things like rope toys and rubber bones. Just make sure that everything you give your puppy to play with is intended for that purpose – don't just throw him one of your child's old stuffed animals, or let him play with something that isn't intended for dogs.

3.) Surviving the First Night with Your Corgi Puppy

So, you have finally brought your Corgi puppy home – now what? It's easy to get caught up in the excitement of making plans for your new puppy, but what do you do with him when you get him home?

What you need to understand about your Corgi puppy is that moving to a new home is going to be frightening for him. It might be his first time away from the rest of his litter, and he may be nervous about it. You might be tempted to give him free-reign of the house, so he can explore his new surroundings, but that might be too overwhelming. It is important to help your puppy settle in, but you need to do it slowly for his own good.

When you first bring your Corgi puppy home, take him to the part of the yard you have designated as his potty area. It's important to establish good potty habits early, and it will make your job of housetraining your puppy easier in the long run. Once your puppy has done his business, give him plenty of praise then take him back inside and let him look around a bit. It's a good idea to limit your puppy's range for a few weeks, but you can still let him explore a little on the first day, so he doesn't become afraid when you eventually expand his range.

After you've given your puppy some time to look around, he's probably going to be ready for a nap. Take him to the area you've set up for him and put him in his crate. If he settles in and takes a nap, great! If he doesn't seem to like the crate, try giving him some praise and a few tasty treats. If all of that fails, just sit down on the couch and hold him in your lap while he falls asleep – this is a good opportunity to start bonding with your new puppy.

Once your puppy wakes from his nap, take him outside again and then give him something to eat. It's a good idea to establish a regular schedule for feeding, so you will be able to predict when your puppy is going to need to go potty. This is also important for housetraining, later on. For the first few feedings, it is best to give your puppy whatever food he was eating before arriving at your home. Once he starts to settle in, you can transition him to a new product if you so choose.

When bedtime comes around, you'll need to follow a couple of rules for the sake of establishing good habits. First and foremost, do NOT take your puppy to bed with you. It is extremely tempting to cuddle with your new puppy, and it may soothe him from whining, but it sets a precedent that you'll have a hard time correcting later. Instead, place your puppy's crate next to your bed and make sure he has a soft plush toy to cuddle with. If he cries during the night, take him outside to do his business, but then put him right back in his crate to go to bed – don't let him play or sniff around too much, and avoid giving him any treats.

Keep in mind that every puppy is different. Some puppies take to the crate right away and may even be able to sleep for a few hours before needing to go out. Other puppies, however, take longer to adjust so you may be in for a few sleepless nights while your puppy whines or howls in the crate by your bed. Do your best not to give in, trusting that your puppy will eventually get used to the crate, and you'll both be able to get a full night's sleep.

CHAPTER 6
Corgi Dog Feeding Guide

Though taking your dog to the vet is very important, there is something else that is likely to have an even greater impact on his health and wellness – his diet. The food you offer your Pembroke Welsh Corgi not only provides him with energy to sustain his metabolism, but also essential nutrients that support bodily functions. All dog foods are NOT created equal, and in reading this chapter, you may find that you know even less about dog food that you thought. Don't worry – we'll cover the basics of understanding your dog's nutritional needs and finding a high-quality, nutritious product to meet those needs.

1.) Understanding Your Corgi's Nutritional Needs

Even if you've never owned a dog before, you probably know the basics about the canine diet. It's all about meat, right? Well, not exactly. Just like you and I, your dog needs a balance of different nutrients in his diet – that means protein, fat, carbohydrates, vitamins, and minerals.

Now, you don't need to memorize a detailed list of nutrients your dog needs, but you should have at least a basic understanding of those needs, so you can shop smart when it comes to choosing a dog food recipe. Let's start with the three macronutrients – protein, fat, and carbohydrates.

Protein is by far the most important nutrient in your dog's diet, and you can probably guess why. That's right; your dog is a carnivore. He may not be a strict carnivore (or obligate carnivore) like a cat is, but the majority of his nutrition should come from animal sources, rather than plants. As a puppy, your puppy requires a minimum of 22% protein in his diet to support healthy growth and development. Once he reaches adulthood, he needs a minimum of 18% protein to maintain lean muscle mass.

Fat is the second most important nutrient in your dog's diet. Now, before you start to question that, consider this – fat is the most calorie-dense of the three macronutrients, which means that it is the most concentrated source of energy. That's right; your Corgi needs plenty of fat in his diet to keep his metabolism running at full speed. In fact, small-breed dogs and active dogs like Corgis need a higher percentage of fat in their diets than larger and more sedentary breeds. Your Corgi's minimum requirement for fat is 8% as a puppy, and 5% as an adult.

Okay, so what about carbohydrates? If you were to ask a canine nutrition expert, he would tell you that dogs do not have specific requirements for carbohydrates in their diet. He might even tell you that carbs have no place in a dog's diet. There are arguments to be made for both sides of the issue, but the fact remains that carbohydrates can provide your Corgi with energy in the form of calories, as well as dietary fiber and essential nutrients.

If you want to feed your Corgi a diet similar to the diet a wild wolf would follow, you might consider a raw food diet. For the average dog owner, however, commercially prepared dog food is the more affordable and convenient option. In most cases, that means that it will contain some kind of carbohydrate. We'll go into greater depth about the best carbs for dogs in the next section but, for now, you should know that protein comes first in order of importance, and fat is essential for meeting your dog's energy needs. Carbohydrates can be beneficial when they come from high-quality sources, but they should not be the focus of your dog's diet.

Aside from protein, fat, and carbohydrates, your dog also needs plenty of fresh water, as well as certain vitamins and minerals. You generally don't need to worry about the specifics of which vitamins and minerals your dog needs because any good dog food product you purchase will already be formulated to meet your Corgi's minimum requirements. How can you be sure? Just look for the AAFCO statement of nutritional adequacy on the label.

The American Association of Feed Control Officials performs a similar role for animal feed and pet food that the FDA performs for human food. AAFCO monitors and regulates the production and sale of commercial pet food products and sets requirements for nutritional minimums. They have established the minimum nutritional requirements for puppies and for adult dogs, so any dog food product you pick from the shelf will state on the label whether it is nutritionally complete. Just make sure you choose a product appropriately designed for your Corgi's life stage – either growth and development (puppy), or maintenance (adult).

2.) Tips for Choosing a Healthy Dog Food

Now that you have a basic understanding of the nutrients your Corgi needs and in what quantity, you're ready to learn how to shop for dog food. You might think that it's as simple as just walking into the pet store and picking a product off the shelf, but it is not. If you want what's best for your Pembroke Welsh Corgi, you need to shop with a discerning eye and compare different options to make the right choice. But how do you tell the difference between a high-quality product and a low-quality product, and what sets the two apart?

You've already learned about the AAFCO statement of nutritional adequacy. Before you buy a bag of dog food, make sure that it is nutritionally complete. Things like meal toppers, treats, and supplements are not nutritionally complete, so you'll see something like this on the label, *"This product is intended for intermittent or supplemental feeding only."* If you're shopping for your dog's staple diet, choose another product.

After checking the AAFCO statement, there are two other parts of the pet food package you should check: the guaranteed analysis and the ingredients list. The guaranteed analysis simply provides a breakdown of the major nutrients in the product – protein, fat, moisture, and fiber. It may also tell you the content of key vitamins and minerals. This is the part of the label you want to look at when making a direct comparison between two products – just make sure you're comparing dry food to dry food or wet food to wet food. If you're trying to cross over, you may need to do some calculations. When making those comparisons, remember the minimum requirements mentioned in the previous section for adults and puppies.

I would argue that the most important part of any pet food package is the ingredients list. When you want to determine whether a food product is good for you, you look at the list of ingredients – the same is true for dog food! In fact, the ingredients list is organized in the same way for pet foods as it is for human food – in descending order by volume. This means that the ingredients at the top of the list are used in the largest quantity. What does that mean? You want to see the healthiest, most high-quality ingredients at the top of the list.

Remember what I said about protein being the most important nutrient for dogs? That's right – you want to see a high-quality source of animal protein as the very first ingredient in any product you choose to feed your dog. Animal proteins are important because they are complete proteins – this means that they contain all of the essential amino acids your dog's body cannot synthesize on its own. Good sources of animal protein for dogs include poultry like chicken or turkey, meat like beef or lamb, fish like salmon or tuna, and eggs. You may also come across products made with game meats like venison, bison, rabbit, or even unconventional proteins, like kangaroo.

After making sure that a high-quality source of animal protein is the first ingredient on the list, you should take a look at the next three to five ingredients, because they're likely to be used in significant quantities, as well. Many dog foods are made with multiple protein sources, so don't be surprised if meat ingredients are the first two or three ingredients on the list. What you do

NOT want to see is some kind of low-quality filler, like corn, wheat, or soy.

Now, what's the problem with corn, wheat, and soy? After all, you eat these foods on a regular basis, and they're considered good for you! What you need to remember is that your dog's digestive system is not optimized for processing plant foods. Plus, corn and wheat products provide very limited nutrition for dogs. If your dog eats any carbohydrates, they should be in the form of whole grains, or fresh fruits and vegetables. Not only are these the most digestible sources of carbohydrate for dogs, but they are also the most nutrient-rich.

Good carbs to see on the ingredients list for dog food include things like whole-grain brown rice, cracked pearled barley, or sweet potato. Many dog foods are grain-free, so you might also see something like tapioca starch or green peas as the primary carbohydrates. You are also likely to see numerous carbohydrate sources included in the list, but just make sure that they don't come before the main source(s) of protein.

Most dog foods worthy of consideration will list a high-quality animal protein first, followed by a digestible carbohydrate or two. Within the first five or six ingredients, you also want to see some kind of healthy fat, to ensure that your dog's needs for energy are met. Healthy fats like salmon oil also provide omega-3 fatty acids which support your dog's immunity, as well as the condition of his skin and coat. Plant-based fats like flaxseed or canola oil can also be fine for dogs, though animal fats like chicken fat and salmon oil are the most nutritious options.

Once you get past the proteins, carbohydrates, and fats, you'll start getting into the supplemental ingredients. Here you'll likely see things like fresh or dried fruits and vegetables, vitamin and mineral supplements, and even probiotics. Fruits and vegetables contribute to the fiber content of a dog food product, but they also provide natural sources of key vitamins and minerals – natural sources are always more biologically valuable for your dog than supplements. So, even though a product made with synthetic vitamins and minerals might be considered nutritionally complete, your dog's body won't be able to absorb the total nutrient content.

Finally, after making sure that the dog food you're looking at contains everything your dog needs, you want to check that it doesn't contain any harmful ingredients. Avoid any product made with artificial flavors, colors, or preservatives and think twice about dog food made with too many supplements – that is a telltale sign that the main ingredients are not of the highest quality. Generally speaking, high-quality products have a shorter list of high-quality ingredients, than low-quality products.

3.) Feeding Tips for Corgi Dogs and Puppies

Using the information from the previous two sections, you have the knowledge you need to choose a healthy and high-quality product for your Pembroke Welsh Corgi. In addition to following that advice, there are a few other things to keep in mind. First and foremost, the Pembroke Welsh Corgi is a small-breed dog, and that means he has slightly different nutritional requirements than a large-breed dog and should be fed a specialized food.

Small-breed dogs have very fast metabolisms, so they need a steadier intake of calories throughout the day and, in most cases, higher fat content in their food to provide those extra calories. So, while the average dog might need about 30 calories per pound of bodyweight per day, small-breed and working breed dogs have a daily requirement closer to 40 calories per pound of bodyweight, per day. For an adult Pembroke Welsh Corgis, that's a range of about 1,000 to 1,200 calories a day.

If you look at the nutritional label on your dog food package, you'll find the calorie content per cup or per kg. You can use that information to determine how much to feed your Corgi – or you could simply follow the feeding recommendations. These recommendations are made according to body weight, so you'll need to know how much your Corgi weighs to determine how much to feed him. Also, keep in mind that these recommendations are usually made for the dog's total daily intake – you'll need to divide it into two or three meals according to your preference.

In addition to choosing a small-breed formula for your Corgi, you should also make sure to feed your puppy a dedicated puppy formula. These recipes are typically higher in both protein and fat to support your puppy's growth and development. You should plan to feed your Corgi puppy a puppy-specific recipe at least until he reaches his full size or 12 months of age, whichever comes first. If you're not sure, ask your vet whether you should keep feeding your Corgi a puppy recipe, or if it is safe to make the switch.

Your Corgi's dog food should be his primary source of nutrition. Any treats you give him are extra and should make up no more than 10% of his daily intake. Keep in mind that you'll be using more treats during training, so consider decreasing your puppy's daily ration a little to compensate, or use his kibble as rewards during training sessions. It's your choice as well whether to give your dog table scraps or not but, if you do, make it an occasional treat and be absolutely sure that everything is safe for dogs like Corgis to eat.

CHAPTER 7

Corgi Socialization Guide

The Pembroke Welsh Corgi is a friendly and fun-loving breed, but they do tend to be a little bit shy around strangers. To make sure that your puppy grows up into a well-adjusted and obedient dog, you need to start as early as possible with both socialization and training. In this chapter, you'll learn how to create a daily schedule for your Corgi, which will be extremely helpful when it comes time for housetraining. You'll also receive some simple tips for socializing your puppy, as well as advice for scheduling play dates and enrolling in puppy classes.

1.) Creating a Schedule for Your Corgi

Dog's thrive on routine, and your Pembroke Welsh Corgi puppy is no different. When you bring your puppy home, it is a good idea to start right away with a consistent feeding schedule.

Puppies need plenty of food to fuel their growth, and this is particularly true for small-breed puppies like your Corgi. You'll want to feed your puppy once in the morning, once in the evening, and one or two additional times during the day. You might also just consider keeping his food bowl full, so he can eat as he gets hungry, but keep in mind that Corgis are highly prone to obesity – if your puppy can't regulate his intake on his own, you'll have to do it for him.

In addition to sticking to a feeding schedule with your puppy, you should start taking him out regularly as well. Always take your puppy out first thing in the morning and the last thing before bed – you should also plan to take him outside about 20 to 30 minutes after a meal. During the in-between times, take your puppy out every hour or two while he is under 2 months old and every two to four hours after that. By the time your puppy reaches six months of age, you should have a pretty good idea how long he can go between potty breaks.

Something else to include in your Pembroke Welsh Corgi puppy's daily routine is playtime. Until your puppy has all of his shots, you should avoid contact with other dogs. So, you might want to exercise him indoors with active play instead of taking him for walks during this period. Playing with your puppy is important for more than just exercise – it also helps you to build a bond with your puppy.

The last thing to include in your puppy's daily schedule is bedtime. Your puppy might spend as many as 16 to 18 hours a day sleeping anyway, but you should try to set a sleep schedule for overnights, just to be sure he sleeps when you sleep. Try to put your puppy to bed in his crate around the same time each night, even if you aren't ready to go to bed yet. You'll probably need to take him out every couple of hours for the first few months but getting him used to spending the night in the crate is important.

You don't necessarily need to schedule every minute of your Corgi puppy's day, but you should try to stick to a routine as much as possible – it will be good for both of you.

2.) Socializing Your Corgi Puppy

During the first few months of his life, your Pembroke Welsh Corgi puppy is going to be very impressionable. While the breed has certain temperament traits, your puppy will still develop his own personality and his own way of viewing and interacting with the world. You can, to some degree, influence these things by exposing your puppy to as many new people, places, and things as possible while he is still young – this is called socialization.

The experiences your puppy has while he is young will shape the way he interacts with the world as an adult. If you expose your puppy to a wide variety of experiences early on, he'll develop greater self-confidence, and he'll be more likely to greet unfamiliar situations as an adult with curiosity, rather than fear. There is a fine line to walk, however, between socializing your puppy and scaring him. He needs to be exposed to things like loud noises, but you don't want to overwhelm him with too many experiences at once.

So, what exactly should you do to socialize your Pembroke Corgi puppy? Here are some general tips:

- Introduce your puppy to new signs, sounds, and smells as much as possible.
- Make sure your puppy experiences things that could be scary – things like the vacuum cleaner or the washing machine.
- Expose your puppy to different indoor and outdoor surfaces including different types of flooring.
- Have your puppy meet as many different kinds of people, as possible. This includes all ages and races.

- Introduce your puppy to other household pets, as long as it is safe to do so.
- Take your puppy out of his comfort zone by taking a ride in the car or walking around the neighborhood.
- Get him a carrying bag, to take him with you as run errands.
- Get your puppy used to wearing different things including collars, harnesses, booties, and sweaters.

As you socialize your puppy via these experiences, make sure you give him plenty of praise – not only do you want your puppy to experience new things, but you want him to experience them in a positive way. Your puppy will take cues from your emotions and behavior as well, so do your best not to act nervous, because it could make your puppy nervous as well.

The best thing you can do to socialize your puppy is to give him as many new experiences as possible. If this is your first dog, however, you may not know exactly what that entails. To help you out, there is a list of some of the things you should expose your puppy to:

- Loud voices
- Laughing
- Crying
- Shouting
- Men
- Women
- Children

- Babies
- Older people
- Wheelchairs
- Strollers
- Wood floors
- Tile
- Linoleum

- Concrete
- Grass
- Sand
- Gravel
- Asphalt
- Cars
- Bicycles
- Traffic
- Car horns
- Sirens
- Fireworks
- Storms
- Rain

- Snow
- Radios
- Parking lots
- Doorbells
- Vet office
- Pet stores
- Kennels
- Small dogs
- Large dogs
- Cats
- Horses
- Ducks

Though you need to expose your puppy to plenty of new things, make sure you don't do too much at once – you don't want to overwhelm your puppy or cause him to form a fearful association with something. Just take your time, be generous with praise and rewards, and have a good time!

3.) Play Dates and Puppy Classes

In addition to socializing your puppy on your own, you should also think about taking him to puppy classes and setting up some puppy play dates. Here are some tips for setting up a puppy play date:

- Know what your puppy does and doesn't like – this will help you plan the playdate and decide what should and shouldn't happen during it.
- Make sure you know how your puppy reacts to other dogs beforehand and choose a puppy that is similar in age, size, and energy level.
- Hold the play date in a neutral location, so neither puppy becomes territorial – make sure it is a safe area for off-leash play as well.
- Keep an eye on your puppy and make adjustments as needed – for example, your puppy and his playmate may not get along well so you might have to cut the date short.
- Let your puppy do his own thing and just sit back and supervise – there's no need to manage the fun, just let the puppies do what they want.

During a puppy play date, it is important to let your puppy and his friend do their own thing. This doesn't mean, however, that you shouldn't (loosely) supervise what's going on. Don't bury your nose in your phone or get caught up in conversation – you need to be able to react quickly if a problem arises.

In addition to setting up puppy play dates, you should also think about enrolling your Pembroke Welsh Corgi puppy in puppy classes. Under six months of age, puppy classes are mainly geared toward socialization and play, though some will help you set the foundation for obedience training. After six months, you may want to look into basic obedience classes. Even if you're working with your puppy at home, a puppy class is a great way to reinforce commands, and it will help your puppy learn to follow instructions in the face of distractions.

CHAPTER 8
Corgi Dog Training

One of the best characteristics of the Pembroke Welsh Corgi breed is his trainability. These dogs are very intelligent, and they learn quickly, though it is your job to teach your dog in a way that enables him to learn. In this chapter, we'll review some of the most common dog training methods, and you'll learn which one is best for the Corgi breed. You'll also learn about the most effective methods for house training your Corgi puppy, and you'll receive tips for dealing with problem behaviors.

1.) Overview of Corgi Training Methods

Though he doesn't exactly compare to the Border Collie in terms of intelligence, the Pembroke Welsh Corgi is still a very smart dog. The higher a dog's intelligence, the more trainable he is – at least, in most cases. That is good news for you because it means that your Corgi will pick up on new commands more quickly. All you have to do is choose the right training method and then use it effectively.

So, what are the different training methods out there? If you were to speak to ten different dog trainers, you might receive ten different recommendations for how to train your Corgi. What you need to think about when evaluating different training methods, is what you are actually teaching your dog and whether you are reinforcing desirable behaviors or discouraging undesirable behaviors.

The training method you choose is completely up to you, but I hope that after about a few different options, you'll make the choice that most dog trainers agree is best.

Let's start with one called "Alpha Dog Training." Even if you haven't heard the phrase Alpha Dog before, you're probably familiar with the concept. This method of training is based on the idea that dogs (like wolves) are pack animals, and it is your job as the dog owner to be the "alpha." This is the training method preferred by the Dog Whisperer Cesar Milan, and it is often used with larger and more aggressive breeds. Neither of those is an accurate description of the Pembroke Welsh Corgi.

You must remember that your Corgi was developed for herding, so his natural instinct is to gather and guard, not to attack. The Alpha Dog method of training often involves forcing the dog to be submissive to the owner, doing things like never letting the dog walk through the door first or forcing him to wait for his dinner until you have finished your own. While some dogs may respond to this kind of training, it is unlikely to be effective with your Corgi. More than that, however, it could negatively impact your relationship with your dog.

So, what is a better option than the Alpha Dog method? Most dog trainers agree that positive reinforcement is the best and most effective method of dog training. This type of training is incredibly simple – you reward your dog for performing desired behaviors and, in doing so, encourage him to repeat them. Dogs are highly motivated by rewards (especially food), so if your Corgi learns that sitting when you ask him to sit earns him a treat, he'll be eager to do it. All you have to do is teach him what the word "sit" means.

We'll talk a little more about positive reinforcement in the next section, but first I want to mention one more style of training that is not recommended. While positive reinforcement is a great way to teach your Corgi to repeat desired behaviors, punishing your dog for undesired behaviors is largely ineffective.

The best example of this is the idea that rubbing your dog's nose is his own "accident" or swatting him with a newspaper will teach him not to do it. In reality, your dog has no idea what you are yelling at him for because the event most likely occurred hours ago while you weren't at home. So, instead of teaching your dog not to have an accident in the house, you're just scaring him by yelling at him, for what seems like no reason. The more you do this, the more likely your dog is to become nervous or even fearful around you. That is not what you want to happen with your Pembroke Welsh Corgi.

2.) Best Training Method for the Welsh Corgi

Now that you know the basics of a few different training methods, you are ready to learn more about the best Corgi training method – positive reinforcement.

As you already learned, positive reinforcement involves rewarding your dog for desired behaviors to increase his likelihood of doing them again. So, if you want your dog to sit when you say sit, reward him for doing it! Keep in mind, however, that no training method will work unless your dog understands what you are asking of him. This means that you have to work with your dog to teach him what the command means first, and then reward him for following it.

So, what does positive reinforcement look like in action?

Here's a sample training sequence for teaching your Corgi puppy to sit:

1. Choose a tasty treat to reward your puppy – you can use his kibble if he'll eat it, or you can choose a tasty morsel for added motivation.

2. Kneel in front of your puppy and hold the treat in your dominant hand – let your puppy sniff it, so he knows it's there.

3. Hold the treat in front of your puppy's nose, just out of reach, and tell him to "sit" in a firm voice.

4. Immediately move the treat forward toward the back of your puppy's head.

5. As your puppy lifts his nose to follow the treat, his bottom should lower to the floor.

6. When your puppy's bottom touches the floor, praise him by telling him, "good sit," and give him the treat.

7. Repeat the sequence a few times until your puppy gets the hang of it, then phase out the food rewards by offering them every other time – continue to praise him each time, however.

As you can see, positive reinforcement training is very simple. You may need to guide your puppy to perform the desired action the first few times, but he'll pick up on it quickly. Just make sure you are consistent about using the same command and giving the reward quickly, so he associates it with the desired behavior.

3.) Corgi House Training Guide

As a dog owner, housetraining is one of your first responsibilities. After all, you don't want to spend the rest of your Pembroke Welsh Corgi's life cleaning up accidents in the house, do you? Fortunately, housetraining is fairly straightforward – you just need a few supplies and some patience.

Here's how you do it:

1. Get your puppy used to his crate and use it to confine him overnight, and when you can't physically watch him.
2. Choose one area of the yard where you want your puppy to do his business – this will make training easier and your task of cleaning up after your puppy simpler, as well.
3. Take your puppy to his potty area first thing in the morning, after meals and naps, and right before bed.
4. Give your puppy a verbal command like "go pee" when you take him to the potty area.
5. If your puppy does his business, praise him and give him a treat – if he doesn't have to pee, take him back inside and try again in 20 minutes.

Doesn't that sound simple? That's because it is. Success with this method of housetraining relies on consistency, however, so make sure you are giving your puppy plenty of opportunities to go outside, and always take him to that same spot. If your puppy has an accident in the house, don't yell at him or punish him – just keep on with your training.

Part of housetraining involves keeping your puppy in his crate overnight. Dogs have a natural aversion to soiling their dens, and your puppy's crate is like his den – if you keep him in it when you can't watch him, it reduces the risk of an accident. Just remember that your Corgi puppy's ability to hold his bladder and bowels will be very limited for a while - he can really only hold it for about an hour for each month of age. This might mean waking up a few times during the night to let him out. Another option is to train him to use puppy pee pads indoors and then transition him to going outdoors later.

4.) Indoor Housetraining for Corgis

If you live in an urban area, or an apartment without access to outdoor space, you might consider indoor housetraining for your Pembroke Welsh Corgi. Before you make this decision, however, you should consider both the good and bad. On the good side, it may be easier than carrying your puppy up and down the stairs. On the bad side, it may be difficult later to train your puppy to go outdoors if you train him to go indoors first.

Though indoor housetraining has its good and bad points, it is an option many dog owners prefer. To do it yourself, you'll have to create a potty space for your puppy. One option is to simply put down an absorbent puppy training pad on the ground and teach your puppy to do his business there. Just follow the same training sequence from the previous section but take your puppy to the pad instead of taking him outdoors. A cleaner option, however, might be to train your puppy to use a litter box.

To create a litter box for your puppy, you can purchase a puppy litter box, or just use a large cat box. Line it with newspaper, puppy training pads, or artificial grass – you can even use cat litter, as long as it is safe for dogs. For convenience, make sure that whatever you line the box with is disposable, or at least easy to clean. Find a place to put the box that is out of the way, but not so far out of the way that your puppy won't use it. From there, you just need to teach him to use the litter box.

Here's how:

1. Introduce your puppy to the litter box and get him used to stepping into and out of it – use treats, if needed, to encourage him.

2. Once your puppy is used to the litter box, start training him to use it.

3. Take your puppy to the litter box first thing in the morning and the last thing before bed – you should also do it after meals and every few hours in between.

4. When you take your puppy to the litter box, give him a verbal command like "go pee" so he learns to associate the command with the action.

5. If your puppy does his business in the box, praise him and reward him, then let him get back to what he was doing before.

The concept of indoor housetraining is very similar to outdoor training, and both methods require consistency. Give your puppy plenty of chances to use the box throughout the day to minimize the risk of accidents, and always praise him for using the box.

5.) Tips for Dealing with Problem Behaviors

In addition to housetraining your dog, you'll also need to learn how to deal with Corgi problems. As you've already learned, punishing your dog for undesirable behavior is rarely effective, and it could have the consequence of damaging your relationship with your dog as well. So, what do you do when your Corgi does something you don't want him to do, like chewing up your favorite pair of shoes or digging holes in the yard?

The best way to deal with Corgi problems like these is to redirect the behavior, rather than trying to stop it entirely. If you think about it, both chewing and digging (as well as other behaviors you might find undesirable), are actually completely normal for a dog. So, if you try to teach your dog to stop these behaviors, he could end up becoming confused or frustrated. Instead, redirect them to a more appropriate outlet.

For example, if your Pembroke Welsh Corgi tends to chew on shoes and other objects, you shouldn't try to teach him not to chew. You should teach him instead, that there are some things he is allowed to chew on and some things he is not. How do you do that? When you find your Corgi chewing on a shoe, tell him "No" in a firm voice (without yelling) and take the shoe away. Immediately replace the shoe with one of your puppy's favorite chew toys, and then praise him when he starts chewing on the toy instead. It's that simple.

This sequence can be used for a variety of problem behaviors. To teach your dog not to dig up your flower beds, for example, you could set aside a corner of the yard where your dog is permitted to dig. Encourage him to do so, by burying treats and toys. But what do you do to curb undesirable behaviors that can't be redirected?

One of the most common problems Corgi owners face is their dogs jumping up on people. What you may not realize is that you probably reinforced this behavior while your Corgi was a puppy – this makes it harder to curb the behavior later. Think about it… what did you do when your cute little Corgi puppy jumped into your lap? You probably greeted him excitedly and gave him plenty of love and attention. In doing so, you inadvertently taught your puppy that this behavior earns him your attention.

So, how do you curb behaviors like these? Just teach your Corgi that the undesirable behavior will not get him what he wants. For example, if your puppy jumps up at your legs, do NOT give him the attention he wants! Tell your puppy "No" or "Off" in a firm voice and stand still, waiting for him to calm down. When he does, praise him and reward him. The more you repeat this sequence, the more your puppy will learn that good behavior earns him your attention (and some tasty treats). You can apply this sequence to a variety of undesirable behaviors.

CHAPTER 9

Corgi Breeding Guide

T he Pembroke Welsh Corgi is a wonderful breed, so no one would blame you for wanting an entire litter of them. What you must realize, however, is that breeding Corgis is a major undertaking and a big responsibility – it should never be done as a hobby or side business. There is no way we can cover absolutely everything you need to know about breeding Corgis, but in this chapter, we'll cover some core information about breeding Corgis and raising Corgi puppies. If you choose to breed your Corgi, you'll need to do some additional research as you go through the process.

1.) Things to Think About Before Breeding Corgis

As tempting as it may be to breed your Corgi, so you can enjoy a litter full of cuddly puppies, think twice about breeding your dog, and then think about it a third time. Dog breeding is a major undertaking, and it is not something that should be done casually or out of a desire to make a little extra money. The truth is that dog breeding is hard work, and it can actually be dangerous for your Corgi if you do it wrong. Here are some things to think about before breeding your Pembroke Welsh Corgi:

- The average litter size for the Corgi breed is 6 to 8 pups – that's a lot of puppies to take care of or find owners for.
- Corgi puppies need a lot of early training and socialization, so you'll have to work with the puppies to make sure they are ready to go to their new homes.

- You probably won't be able to keep the entire litter of puppies and letting them go can be hard, especially if you've grown attached to them.

- Breeding dogs is not just time-consuming, it is also expensive – you have to pay for food as well as vet costs for the mother, as well as the puppies.

- Corgis are prone to a number of inherited health problems that can be passed on through breeding if you aren't careful.

- Giving birth can be difficult for many Corgis because their pelvises are narrow– many Corgis must deliver by C-section.

You should also think about the fact that before breeding your Corgi, you'll have to forgo spaying or neutering – this choice comes with risks of its own. In female dogs, spaying will help to prevent uterine infections and breast tumors. In male dogs, neutering can help prevent testicular cancer and various prostate problems.

2.) Corgi Dog Breeding Information

Now that you know a little more about the risks associated with breeding Pembroke Welsh Corgis, let's talk a little more about the actual breeding process. Though each dog breed is unique, the basics of breeding are the same – it all has to do with the estrous cycle.

The estrous cycle is the part of the female reproductive cycle during which a dog can become pregnant – it is also sometimes known as the "heat" cycle. Smaller dogs like Corgis typically have their first cycle around six months of age, though it can happen earlier. Once a Corgi becomes sexually mature, she will go through the heat cycle about every six months, though it is possible for smaller dogs to have as many as three heat cycles per year.

The average heat cycle for the Pembroke Welsh Corgi lasts about 2 to 3 weeks. At the start of the cycle, you may notice symptoms such as swelling of the external vulva followed by vaginal discharge. Over the course of several days, the discharge will change from being red and bloody to being watery and pink – this usually happens over the course of about 10 days. During the heat cycle, a female dog may also develop marking behavior, urinating on objects in the home, or on walks to leave her scent.

A male dog can detect a female dog in heat from a great distance, so you need to be very careful about monitoring your Corgi when she is in heat, to prevent accidental breeding. Always keep your dog on a leash when walking her and avoid dog parks and any areas where other dogs might be present. It is also a bad idea to leave her in the yard alone, fenced or not.

Around the time the dog's vaginal discharge becomes watery is when she is the most fertile and receptive to breeding – this is when you would introduce the male dog. Many dog breeders allow multiple breeding sessions during each heat to increase the chances of a successful pregnancy. You should also keep in mind that sperm can survive for up to a week in the female Corgi's reproductive tract, so she can technically become pregnant at any time during the cycle, not just when she is most fertile.

If breeding is successful and your Pembroke Welsh Corgi becomes pregnant, she will enter the gestation period – the period of time during which the puppies develop in the womb. Pregnancy usually lasts 63 days or about 9 weeks for dogs, and you may not be able to detect the pregnancy until the third week. After about 28 days, an experienced vet will be able to palpate the uterus to detect pregnancy, and an ultrasound can be safely performed after about 25 days. Around 6 weeks is when the puppies' skeletons become calcified and can be picked up by x-rays if you want to see how big the litter will be.

During the last week of pregnancy, you want to provide your female Pembroke Welsh Corgi with a comfortable place to nest. Keep in mind that delivery will be messy, so provide some old towels and blankets that you can simply throw away after. Start keeping an eye out for the signs of labor as well so you can be ready when it happens. Just in case there is a problem, you will need to call the vet. Here is what you can expect when your dog goes into labor:

- A dog's normal body temperature is between 101°F and 102.5°F – when it drops below 100°F, labor will start within 24 hours.
- During the first stage of labor, your dog's cervix will dilate, and uterine contractions will start.
- Your dog will become increasingly agitated and uncomfortable as contractions begin – she may pant, shiver, and pace, and might whine as well.
- The average labor lasts for 16 to 18 hours for a dog, and you should keep your dog in a calm, quiet environment for the duration.
- During the second stage of labor, contractions intensify, and the placental water sacks will break.
- When delivery begins, the pups are usually birthed every 30 minutes after 10 to 30 minutes of forceful straining – after delivery, the mother will lick the puppies clean.

Because Corgi deliveries can be tricky, it is a good idea to supervise the proceedings. It is not uncommon for a dog to take a rest that lasts for more than 30 minutes between puppies. But if 4 hours pass with no delivery, and you are certain there are more puppies, take your dog to the vet.

3.) Tips for Raising Corgi Puppies

Once delivery is complete comes the fun part – raising your new Pembroke Welsh Corgi puppies! When they are first born, Corgi puppies usually weigh about 10 ounces, though they can range from as small as 6 ounces to as large as 18 ounces. Puppies are born with their eyes and ears closed, so they are completely dependent on their mother – they even rely on her licking them to stimulate breathing and circulation. The hours after birth are also when the mother bonds with her puppies and learns to recognize them.

Until about two weeks of age, your Pembroke Welsh Corgi puppies will be blind and deaf. They won't have any teeth, and they will be unable to regulate their own body temperatures. They will spend most of their time feeding and sleeping. Around 2 to 4 weeks of age is when their eyes begin to open, and they start responding to their surroundings. This is also when the puppies develop the ability to eliminate without their mother's help.

After about 3 to 4 weeks of age, your puppies will become more alert and aware of their surroundings, and they may even begin to recognize you. It is important to be gentle with the puppies during this stage because they are extremely impressionable. After about 4 weeks you can begin socialization – make sure your puppies have plenty of human interaction and handle them often, so they get used to being around people. This is also when the puppies will learn bite inhibition from playing with their littermates, and they may start to sample solid food as well.

At 8 weeks your Pembroke Welsh Corgi puppies may go through a second socialization stage during which they become fearful of just about everything, even things they were fine with before. During this time, you should avoid loud noises and traumatic events, but keep giving the puppies plenty of human interaction. Your puppies should also be mostly transitioned onto eating solid food by this point which means that they are ready to go to their new homes if you can find them.

Over the next few months, puppies will develop their personalities a little bit, and they'll become more outgoing and inquisitive. Pembroke Welsh Corgis are naturally intelligent and curious dogs, so you'll have to keep a close eye on your puppy during this stage to keep him out of trouble. You may not be able to do much obedience training because he will probably be too high-strung, but you can set the stage for obedience training by enforcing house rules, and you can set the stage for housetraining as well. Refer to Chapter 8 for a more detailed guide on housetraining.

CHAPTER 10
Corgi Health Guide

T he Pembroke Welsh Corgi is generally a fairly healthy breed with an average lifespan of 12 to 14 years. Even so, all dogs are prone to developing certain health problems, and it is your job as a dog owner to know what those potential problems are and how to identify them. In this chapter, you'll learn about the most common health problems to which the Pembroke Welsh Corgi is prone and how they are treated. You'll also receive some valuable information about vaccinating your dog and whether you should consider purchasing pet insurance.

1.) Common Corgi Health Problems

As you have already learned, all dogs are prone to developing certain health problems over the course of their lives. These health problems can be influenced by a number of factors including genetics, diet, and lifestyle. Feeding your Pembroke Welsh Corgi a high-quality diet is the best thing you can do to protect his health for the long-term, but you should still be aware of the conditions to which the breed is prone.

The more you know about potential health concerns, the more prepared you will be in case something should happen. You should be aware of the symptoms to look out for and, if your dog does get sick, you'll want to seek veterinary treatment as soon as possible. The earlier you catch the problem, and seek treatment, the better your Corgi's chances are of making a full recovery.

So, what kind of health problems are known to affect the Pembroke Welsh Corgi breed? Here is a list:

- Cataracts
- Cutaneous asthenia
- Cystinuria
- Degenerative Myelopathy
- Epilepsy
- Hip dysplasia
- Intervertebral disk disease
- Patent ductus arteriosus
- Progressive retinal atrophy
- Von Willebrand's disease

Keep reading to learn more about each of these diseases including the symptoms, causes, and treatment options.

A. Cataracts

In dogs as well as humans, a cataract is an opacity of the lens of the eye that can cause blurry vision. When the cataract is small, it may not affect your Corgi's vision significantly, but it needs to be monitored because it could become denser and thicker over time which could lead to eventual blindness. In most cases, cataracts are the result of an inherited condition, though they can also be related to old age or trauma to the eye. Diagnosis of cataracts can be made through an eye exam.

Cataracts are pretty easy to identify – they look like a cloudy, bluish gray area on the eye. Keep in mind that it is normal for a Corgi's eyes to cloud a little bit with age, but you should still have him checked out by a vet to be safe. Unfortunately, cataracts can't be cured medically, but they can be surgically removed. Cataract surgery in dogs has a high success rate, and most dogs recover very well, though the procedure does necessitate some pretty extensive postoperative care.

B. Cutaneous Asthenia

Also known as Ehlers-Danlos syndrome, cutaneous asthenia in Pembroke Welsh Corgis occurs when the skin becomes unusually stretchy or droopy. This disease is part of a group of inherited conditions that arise due to genetic mutation, and the dogs who have it are deficient in collagen in their skin. Collagen is a type of protein that helps give skin its strength and elasticity – without it, the skin will droop, and it may become prone to tearing. This is a fairly rare disease; but unfortunately, Corgis are one of the breeds most likely to get it.

Symptoms of cutaneous asthenia in Corgis include excess folds of skin, soft or delicate skin, saggy skin, frequent skin tears or scarring, swollen joints, bruising or bleeding under the skin, and internal bleeding. This condition is entirely hereditary and caused by a genetic mutation and even dogs that don't show symptoms can pass the disease to their offspring. There are no treatments currently available, though some therapies may make your dog more comfortable. When the condition becomes painful, however, euthanasia may be the best option.

C. Cystinuria

Typically referred to as canine cystinuria, this disease affects your Corgi's kidneys – it prevents them from filtering cystine out of the urine as well as they should. When the kidneys fail to filter out the cystine, it accumulates in the urine where it crystalizes and forms calculi or kidney stones. Cystinuria is caused by a genetic mutation, but not every dog who has this mutation will display symptoms of the disease. Dogs that do show symptoms are more likely to be male due to their long, narrow urethra.

Symptoms of cystinuria in Pembroke Welsh Corgis may include bloody urine, frequent urination, painful urination and straining to urinate. If the stones pass into the urethra, they could cause a blockage which can trigger acute kidney failure – symptoms of this include vomiting, loss of appetite, and lethargy. Treatment depends on the severity of the condition. If there is a blockage, surgery is the most common treatment, but dietary changes, nutritional supplements, and medications may be enough to reduce smaller stones or to prevent their formation.

D. Degenerative Myelopathy

This disease is a progressive spinal disorder that is similar to ALS or Lou Gehrig's disease in humans. Degenerative myelopathy (DM) most commonly affects older dogs and symptoms typically manifest around the age of 8 years or older. These symptoms progress slowly over the course of several months or years, culminating in paraplegia, or hind leg paralysis. Fortunately, most dogs remain alert and animated during this progression.

In the early stages of DM, you may notice subtle signs like loss of coordination, dragging the hind feet, or hind end weakness. These symptoms may progress to include knuckling of the hind feet, difficulty supporting the weight with the back legs, incontinence, and inability to walk without support. Eventually, the hind legs will become completely paralyzed, and the front legs may weaken as well. Degenerative myelopathy is genetically inherited, and there is no treatment currently available to alter the course of the disease significantly.

E. Epilepsy

In dogs and humans, epilepsy is a condition characterized by frequent seizures. It is a lifelong disease that requires regimented care and treatment. A seizure happens when an abnormal electrical impulse in the brain causes a sudden but short-lived disturbance in the dog's behavior and movements. Potential causes of seizures include trauma, brain tumors, toxin exposure, infections, and problems with the blood or organs. With epileptic seizures, the dog may or may not lose consciousness.

Some of the most common symptoms of epilepsy in dogs include paddling the legs, collapsing or falling to one side, excessive drooling or foaming, frenzied whining or barking, head shaking, incontinence, and loss of consciousness. There are several different types of epilepsy and different triggers for seizures – it is important to identify your dog's triggers and to avoid them as much as possible. Though epilepsy is a chronic condition, treatment is possible through medication and dietary changes. Limiting your dog's salt intake and keeping his diet consistent, are two dietary changes that might help.

F. Hip Dysplasia

One of the most common musculoskeletal conditions to affect dogs, hip dysplasia, is the result of a deformity in the hip that occurs during a puppy's growth period. The hip joint consists of a ball and sock – for healthy function, both the ball and socket must grow at equal rates. If uniform growth is inhibited, the joint may be lax, and the resulting degenerative joint disease or osteoarthritis may develop as the body's attempt to stabilize the joint. Unfortunately, these arthritic changes can be painful and may cause lameness in the affected limb.

There are two potential causes of hip dysplasia – diet and genetics. Though the exact genes responsible for hip dysplasia have not yet been identified, it is thought that there is more than one. In terms of diet and its effects on hip dysplasia, large-breed puppies need to be fed a diet that won't encourage overgrowth

– free feeding has also been associated with higher rates of hip dysplasia. Symptoms of this condition include pain and weakness in the hind legs as well as a wobbly gate or reluctance to rise. Treatment may include NSAID pain relievers, moderate exercise, and physical therapy. When those don't work, surgery is an option to replace or repair the hip.

G. Intervertebral Disk Disease

Also known as IVDD, intervertebral disk disease in dogs is often characterized by a slipped or herniated disk. The disks are simply the pads between the vertebrae that act as shock-absorbers to cushion the spine. If one or more disks becomes displaced or if it deteriorates, collapses, or bulges, it can be very painful. Symptoms may include reluctance to move, stiffness, sensitivity to touch, arched back, dragging legs, and inability to stand. This is one of the most common neurological disorders in dogs, affecting about 2% of the domestic dog population overall.

There are two types of IVDD in dogs – Hansen Type I and Hansen Type II. Both of these involve degeneration of the intervertebral disks, but the cause and mechanism of that degeneration are different. In Type I, acute herniation comes on suddenly and affects chondrodystrophic breeds like the Corgi. Type II comes on more slowly and usually affects nonchondrodystrophic breeds. Treatment for this condition usually involves plenty of rest along with medical management or, in more severe cases, surgical intervention to correct the problem.

H. Patent Ductus Arteriosus

This is a congenital defect that affects the ductus arteriosus, the arterial shunt located between the aorta and the pulmonary artery – these are the two primary blood vessels that lead from the heart. This shunt is normally present during fetal development, and it is what allows blood to bypass the lungs since the fetus receives all the oxygen it needs through the placenta. When the puppy is born and takes its first breath, the ductus arteriosus is stimulated to close which allows blood to circulate through the lungs. When the ductus arteriosus fails to close after birth, it causes the disease known as patent ductus arteriosus.

When this happens, there is a significant difference in pressure between the aorta and the pulmonary artery which causes the blood to flow through the patent ductus arteriosus into the pulmonary artery where it is needlessly recirculated back through the lungs. Because less blood flows through the aorta, the left side of the heart has to work harder, and it eventually leads to congestive heart failure. Symptoms of PDA include difficulty breathing, heart murmur, abnormal heart rhythm, and exercise intolerance. In most cases, surgery can repair the problem.

I. Progressive Retinal Atrophy

The name progressive retinal atrophy (PRA) is actually given to a group of degenerative eye disorders that eventually lead to blindness in both eyes. Though the exact cause is not known, it is commonly thought that PRA is a genetic condition. Early symptoms of PRA include night blindness as well as a reluctance to go downstairs or to navigate unfamiliar areas. As the disease progresses, the surface of the eye becomes cloudy and gray.

Progressive blindness may cause the dog to bump into furniture, or stumble over objects.

In most cases, PRA is not painful, and dogs typically adjust well to a loss of vision. Unfortunately, there is no treatment for the disease, and you cannot prevent it if your Corgi is a carrier. Once the degeneration starts, you cannot stop it, so your best bet is to keep your dog's environment as stable as possible. This condition shouldn't affect your dog's health in any other way, so he can live a perfectly full and happy life even if he loses his vision.

J. Von Willebrand Disease

Sometimes shortened to vWD, von Willebrand disease is the most common inherited blood clotting disorder to affect dogs. This disease is the result of insufficient von Willebrand Factor (vWF), a type of plasma protein that helps the blood to clot. Without vWF, your Corgi may bleed excessively from even minor injuries. There are three types of von Willebrand disease which range in severity and symptoms are usually only noticeable in the more severe cases. Symptoms may include unexplained bleeding from the mouth or nose as well as blood in the stool or urine, anemia, and excessive bleeding from minor injury.

Unfortunately, there is no cure for von Willebrand disease, but the condition can be managed. The goal of treatment is to control bleeding and to stop it as soon as possible when it happens. This may also involve correcting underlying conditions that contribute to vWD. If your dog needs surgery, he may require a blood transfusion to reduce surgical risks, but the disease may not significantly impact his day-to-day life.

2.) Corgi Vaccinations and Precautions

As much as you might wish you could, you can't completely protect your Pembroke Welsh Corgi from getting sick. All dogs are prone to certain health problems, as you well know from reading the previous section. There are, however, certain things you can do to reduce your dog's risk of getting sick – vaccinations are one of them. Vaccines exist for some of the most common communicable canine diseases, and you can get them at your local veterinarian's office.

When Corgis are born, their immune systems are not fully developed – they rely on antibodies from the mother to keep them safe during their first few weeks of life. Starting around six to eight weeks of age, however, you'll be able to have your puppy vaccinated against common diseases like distemper, parvovirus, adenovirus, and parainfluenza. As your Corgi gets older, you will also be able to vaccinate him for rabies, Bordetella, Lyme Disease, and leptospirosis. Your veterinarian may also recommend additional vaccines if the risk for certain diseases is high in your area.

So, when do you start taking your puppy to the vet? Before you can answer this question, you need to know whether your puppy has already seen a vet or been given any vaccinations by the breeder. When you purchase a Corgi puppy, you should be given a copy of his health records as well – bring them with you when you go to the vet for the first time. It's usually a good idea to have your puppy seen by the vet you intend to use, within a week or so of bringing him home. Your vet will tell you then what kind of vaccines he needs and recommend a schedule.

Though each vet does things differently, here is a general vaccination schedule for puppies and dogs you can use for your own reference:

Vaccination Schedule for Corgis			
Vaccine	**Doses**	**Age**	**Booster**
Rabies (US only)	1	12 weeks	annual
Distemper	3	6-16 weeks	3 years
Parvovirus	3	6-16 weeks	3 years
Adenovirus	3	6-16 weeks	3 years
Parainfluenza	3	6 weeks, 12-14 weeks	3 years
Bordetella	1	6 weeks	annual
Lyme Disease	2	9, 13-14 weeks	annual
Leptospirosis	2	12 and 16 weeks	annual
Canine Influenza	2	6-8, 8-12 weeks	annual

3.) Should You Consider Pet Insurance?

Though the Pembroke Welsh Corgi is a fairly healthy breed, there are no guarantees. Your dog could be carrying a genetic condition, and you might not know until years down the line. At the same time, accidents can also happen that might injure your dog and leave you saddled with expensive vet bills. So, what are your options?

One option is to simply take your dog to the vet as needed and pay for his care. Another option is to purchase a pet insurance policy. Pet insurance is similar to health insurance, but there are some key differences you need to understand before you buy.

First of all, know that there are different kinds of pet insurance – some policies cover accidents and injuries while others only cover preventive care or specific treatments. You'll need to do your research to determine what kind of plan offers the coverage you want and then make your decision. You should also be wary of any per-incident or per-annum deductibles or limits. This means that you may have to pay a deductible every time you use your benefits, or your benefits may be limited to a certain dollar amount for each incident, or per year.

Something else to consider is that, like health insurance, most pet insurance plans do not cover pre-existing conditions. You might also find that some companies charge more for dogs over a certain age, or for certain breeds, depending on the diseases to which they are prone. Again, be sure to shop around before you make your choice about pet insurance.

Finally, know that the way pet insurance provides benefits is very different from the way your health insurance plan probably works. While your health insurance plan probably makes payments directly to your provider, most pet insurance plans operate by reimbursement. You will likely still have to pay veterinary costs upfront, but the plan will reimburse you at a certain percentage – that percentage may vary, so be sure to read the fine print.

Pet insurance definitely is not the right choice for everyone. There is always the possibility that you will pay your monthly premiums and then never end up using your benefits – that could be hundreds or thousands of dollars down the drain. On the other hand, your dog could develop a serious disease like cancer that requires expensive treatment – treatment you might not be able to afford without pet insurance. In the end, you need to look at the numbers, research your options, and make the decision that is best for you and your dog.

CHAPTER 11

Corgi Dog Show Guide

When you think of The Westminster Dog Show or Cruft's, you probably picture a giant show ring full of big, beautiful dogs with long silky coats. Though the Pembroke Welsh Corgi may not meet this description, he belongs in the show ring just as much as any Afghan Hound. Showing your dog is a challenging but rewarding experience, and it's most definitely something to consider. In this chapter, you'll learn about the breed standard for the Pembroke Welsh Corgi according to different kennel clubs, and you'll receive some practical tips for showing your dog as well.

1.) Pembroke Welsh Corgi Breed Standard

Before you even think about showing your Pembroke Welsh Corgi, you need to make sure that he is a good example of the breed standard. What is a breed standard? It is simply a set of guidelines for how a specific breed should look and act according to a specific breed club. These standards may vary slightly from one club to another, so make sure your dog meets the standards, for the club you want to show him under.

Keep reading to review the breed standard for the Pembroke Welsh Corgi according to the American Kennel Club, the United Kennel Club, and The Kennel Club (UK).

A. American Kennel Club Standard

General Appearance and Temperament

The Pembroke Welsh Corgi is a low-set, sturdily built dog with great stamina and substance. He should not appear coarse or overdone, nor light-boned or racy. His expression is intelligent and interested, his temperament bold and kind, never shy or vicious.

Head and Face

The head is foxy in both shape and appearance with a fairly-wide skull flat between the ears. The muzzle is neither Roman-nosed or dish-faced, the eyes oval and medium in size, brown in harmony with the coat color. The ears are erect and firm, medium in size and tapering to a rounded point. The neck is fairly long and slightly arched.

Body and Tail

The dog has a well-sprung ribcage, slightly egg-shaped with a deep chest well let down between the forelegs. The topline is firm and level, the tail docks as short as possible, without becoming indented. A natural dock is permissible as long as it is sufficiently short. A tail length of up to two inches is acceptable.

Legs and Feet

The legs are short with the forearms turned slightly inward. The feet are oval with the two middle toes slightly advanced of the two outer toes, turning neither in nor out. The nails are short, the dewclaws removed, and the pads are strong.

Coat and Color

The coat is medium in length, short and thick with a weather-resistant undercoat, and a coarse, medium-length topcoat. Coat length varies over the body, being slightly longer and thicker in the ruff around the neck as well as the chest and shoulders. A straight coat is preferable, though some waviness may be permitted. Color is to be self-colored in red, sable, fawn, black, or tan with or without white markings. White body color and bluish cast are serious faults, as are mismarks.

Size and Gait

The ideal height is 10 to 12 inches to the withers and weight in proportion to size, not exceeding 30 pounds for males and 28 pounds for females. The proportion is moderately long and low, the gait free and smooth. As a herding dog, the breed should have the endurance, agility, and freedom of movement to do the work for which he was developed.

Faults and Disqualifications

The dog will be severely penalized for being oversized or undersized, having a button nose, or drop ears, having an overshot or undershot bite, being overly fluffy or feathered, being mismarked, or his coat having a bluish tint or having a white coat with red or dark markings. Dogs should never be shy or vicious.

B. United Kennel Club Standard

General Appearance and Temperament

The Pembroke Welsh Corgi gives the appearance of substance and stamina in a small space due to his strong, low-set, and sturdy build. He is alert and active, bold in outlook, and neither shy nor vicious.

Head and Face

The heady is foxy in both shape and appearance, the skull fairly wide and flat between the ears. There is a moderate snout, and the cheeks are slightly rounded. The muzzle is somewhat tapered, the teeth strong with a scissors bite, and the eyes medium and oval in shape. Eye color is brown, blending with the color of the coat, the nose black and fully pigmented. The ears are medium in size, firm, and erect, tapering to a slightly rounded point. The neck is fairly long and slightly arched, blending to the shoulders.

Body and Tail

The body is medium in length with well-sprung ribs, tapering slightly when viewed from above. The chest is deep and broad with a level topline and strong, flexible hindquarter. The tail is short, either docked or naturally bobbed, set on line with the topline.

Legs and Feet

The forelegs are short and straight; the elbows fit close to the body. The hind legs are short with ample bone, the rear pasterns parallel when viewed from behind. The feet are arched with short nails and strong pads, turning neither in nor out. The feet are oval-shaped with the center two toes slightly longer than the outer two.

Coat and Color

The coat is medium length and double, straight with a good texture. The coat length varies, being slightly longer and thicker on the chest and shoulders, as well as the ruff around the neck. The hair on the body lies flat and straight, though a slight wave is permitted. Acceptable colors include self-colors of red, sable, fawn, black, and tan, with or without white markings. Also permissible are white markings on the chest, neck, legs, muzzle, and a narrow blaze is also accepted.

Size and Gait

The height measured to the withers should be 10 to 12 inches, the weight in proportion to size but not to exceed 30 pounds for males and 28 pounds for females. Gait should be free and smooth.

Faults and Disqualifications

Serious faults include a rolling or high-stepping gait and short, chopping movement. Other faults include oversize or undersize; whities, bluies, or fluffies; curled tail; feet too round or long; bat ears; and black, yellow, or bluish eyes. Disqualifications include albinism, and extreme shyness or viciousness.

C. The Kennel Club (UK) Standard

The breed standard for the Pembroke Welsh Corgi according to The Kennel Club is much less detailed than the standards set by the AKC and the UKC. Here is a summary of points from The Kennel Club standard for the Pembroke Welsh Corgi Breed:

- General appearance is strong, low-set, and sturdily built, to give an impression of substance and stamina.
- The temperament is outgoing and friendly and a bold outlook.
- The head is foxy in shape with an alert, intelligent expression in well set, round, medium-sized eyes brown in color.
- The ears are medium-sized, pricked, and slightly rounded.
- The jaws are strong with a regular, scissors bite.
- The lower legs are short and as straight as possible, the hindquarters strong and flexible.

- The tail is short and preferable natural; both undocked and docked tails are permissible.
- The gait is free and active, the forelegs moving well forward without much lift.
- The coat is medium in length, straight with a dense undercoat – it is neither soft nor wavy or wiry.
- Permissible colors include self-colors of red, sable, fawn, black, and tan, with or without white markings.
- The height is 25 to 30 cm (10 to 12 inches) at the shoulder, weight 10 to 12 kg (22 to 26 pounds for dogs, 20 to 24 pounds for bitches).

Any departure from these points is considered a fault and the seriousness will be in proportion to the degree of fault and its effect on the health and welfare of the dog, as well as its ability to perform its job.

2.) Tips for Showing AKC Corgi Dogs

If you have your heart set on showing your Pembroke Welsh Corgi, you need to not only determine that he is a good specimen of the breed, but you must also review the requirements for whatever club you plan to go through. Individual requirements will vary from one show to another but, for most shows, your dog should meet the following general requirements:

- He should be at least 1 year old (unless you are showing him in the puppy class).
- He must be housetrained for at least 6 hours.
- He should be properly socialized and comfortable in a crowded, noisy setting.
- He must be an excellent example of the breed according to the relevant club's breed standard.
- He should have plenty of obedience training and respond to commands even in a distracting setting.
- He must be up-to-date on all vaccinations, especially rabies and Bordetella.
- His coat must be natural and in good condition, meeting the requirements of the breed standard.
- He should be properly groomed, including trimmed nails and clean ears.

As long as your Pembroke Welsh Corgi meets these requirements and fulfills the tenants of the breed standard, you can move forward and start looking at the requirements for the specific show you plan to enter him in.

Read through the requirements very carefully and make sure you submit your registration on time. Be sure to bring a copy of your registration with you, as well as some basic supplies – here is a quick list of things to bring:

- Registration information
- Your dog's identification including license number and rabies vaccination info (US only)
- A dog crate and/or exercise pen
- A grooming table and any necessary grooming supplies or equipment
- Food, water, and treats for the entire day (for both you and your dog)
- Bowls for your dog's food and water
- Toys to keep your dog occupied

- Any medications your dog may need
- Paper towels, plastic gloves, and trash bags for after-show cleanup
- A change of clothes, just in case

When you show your Corgi for the first time, you should view it as a learning experience – do not enter the show ring for the first time expecting to win. This is not to say that it isn't possible, but showing your dog is a skill that takes time to learn. It will be a learning experience for your dog as well! Take the opportunity to observe and learn from other dog owners as well, and don't be afraid to ask questions during or after judging, as long as the judge will allow you to do so.

CHAPTER 12

Pembroke Welsh Corgi Trusted Resource List

- Pembroke Welsh Corgi Club of America, Inc.
  http://pwcca.org/

- Breed Standard – Pembroke Welsh Corgi. The Kennel Club.
  https://www.thekennelclub.org.uk/services/public/breed/
  standard.aspx?id=5145

- Calista Corgis, New York Based Breeder, AKC Merit Breeder
  http://www.calistacorgi.com

- Cascade Pembroke Welsh Corgi Club.
  https://cpwcc.org/

- Dogs: Positive Reinforcement Training. The Humane Society.
  http://www.humanesociety.org/animals/dogs/tips/dog_
  training_positive_reinforcement.html

- How to Understand a Dog or Cat Food Label. AAFCO.
  https://talkspetfood.aafco.org/readinglabels

- Jimanie Pembroke Welsh Corgis
  http://www.welshcorgi.com

- Marnac Pembrokes, Breeder, based in Kansas City Missouri.
  http://www.marnacpembrokes.com

- Misty Ridge Pembroke Welsh Corgis, Breeder, based in
  Colorado
  http://www.mistyridgecorgis.com/

- Nistler's Farm Corgis, Family Based Breeder located in
  Missouri
  https://www.farmcorgis.com/

- Pembroke Welsh Corgi. American Kennel Club.
  http://www.akc.org/dog-breeds/pembroke-welsh-corgi

- Merck Vet Manual
  https://www.merckvetmanual.com

- Vaccarella Corgis, Upstate New York family Pembroke Welsh Corgi breeders
  http://vaccarellacorgis.com

- "Your Puppy Socialization Checklist." Pet Professional Guild.
  https://www.petprofessionalguild.com/Resources/
  Documents/PPG-Client-Puppy-Socialization-Download.pdf

Made in the USA
Middletown, DE
30 October 2020

22983932R00075